T0198704

UNDERSTANDING
Your Gifted Child
From the Inside Out

UNDERSTANDING
Your Gifted Child
From the Inside Out

A Guide to the Social and
Emotional Lives of Gifted Kids

James R. Delisle, Ph.D.

Routledge
Taylor & Francis Group

NEW YORK AND LONDON

Library of Congress Cataloging-in-Publication Data

Names: Delisle, James R., 1953- author.
Title: Understanding your gifted child from the inside out : a guide to the
  social and emotional lives of gifted kids / James R. Delisle, Ph.D.
Other titles: Parenting gifted kids.
Description: Waco, TX : Prufrock Press Inc., [2018] | Revised edition of the
  author's Parenting gifted kids, c2006. | Includes bibliographical
  references.
Identifiers: LCCN 2018031974 (print) | LCCN 2018043510 (ebook) | ISBN
  9781618218094 (eBook) | ISBN 9781618218087 (pbk.)
Subjects: LCSH: Gifted children. | Parents of gifted children. | Parenting. |
  Gifted children--Education. | Education--Parent participation.
Classification: LCC HQ773.5 (ebook) | LCC HQ773.5 .D443 2018 (print) | DDC
  649/.155--dc23
LC record available at https://lccn.loc.gov/2018031974

First published in 2018 by Prufrock.Press Inc.

Published in 2021 by Routledge
605 Third Avenue, New York, NY 10017
2 Park Square, Milton Park, Abingdon, Oxon OX14 4RN

Routledge is an imprint of the Taylor & Francis Group, an informa business.

ISBN: 9781618218087 (pbk)

DOI: 10.4324/9781003239352

Dedication

To the world's two best mothers—my own,
Marie Delisle, and my wife, Deb Delisle.

If I am a good dad, it is due to their gentle lessons
about what it means to be a parent.

Table of Contents

Introduction

Parents are funny people. They bring kids into this world despite having virtually no training on what to do to make certain that their children will be happy, successful, and kind. Untold money is spent, and countless sleepless nights are endured, all in the hope that, at some distant time, our progeny will become independent and self-sufficient. Books abound on what mileposts kids should achieve by a certain age, and whether the benchmark involves height, weight, or learning the ABCs, parents are always on the lookout for indicators that their kids are growing. We are the custodians of our children's legacy, at least for a while, and we want to do all we can to set them on a fulfilling life trajectory.

This parenting situation becomes even more precarious when the child in question deviates in some significant ways from one who is developing on a typical timeline. For instance, if a child has a cognitive delay or a physical disability, expectations for "what will happen when" don't fit into the Dr. Spock playbook on child rearing. Modifications need to be made to fit the child's needs and abilities. The same is true when a child shows signs of precocious development—giftedness—and is capable of advanced thoughts or a deep understanding of the human condition at a very young age. Where does a parent turn when her son starts reading billboards from the back seat at age 2, or his daughter asks, at age 5, to have the TV channel changed because "the news is too sad tonight"?

There are lots of books and experts offering advice on navigating the parenting waters and raising kids like yours, be they average or veering off in one direction or other from the norm. And yes, this is one of those books, albeit one that is focused on gifted children. But here's how I hope my book is different from the many others that exist on parenting strategies: I want to offer something more complete and complex than a set of tips and strategies that address an immediate issue or problem. I want to put into a larger context the many moving parts that constitute the lives of gifted children and the people who are raising them; I want to offer guidance in distinguishing whether certain traits and behaviors of gifted children have something to do with their advanced abilities or are mere expressions of their individuality; and I want to help parents of gifted children feel comfortable with the uncomfortable fact that some people just don't care that their kids have advanced intellectual abilities. In essence, I want my book to provide as much solace as it does advice because, let's be honest, parenting a gifted child in a world that neither fully accepts nor appreciates advanced abilities in kids can be an unkind and lonely task at times—for you, as well as for the gifted child who brought you to pick up this book in the first place.

In writing this book, I bring with me more than 40 years of experience as an educator, counselor, and dad of gifted children. This doesn't mean I have all of the answers, but it *does* mean that I have enjoyed thousands of interactions with gifted kids and those who care about them that have informed my thoughts. In sharing some of these experiences with you through this book, I hope that together, as reader and author, we can forge paths that lead to some intriguing outcomes and insights.

Parents are funny people because they willingly take the greatest risk that an individual can take: shaping the lives of those who will eventually shape the lives of others. Let the journey begin. . . .

—Jim Delisle

Chapter 1

Understand What Giftedness Is . . . and What It Is Not

At a meeting with Jeff's mom and several of his teachers, including me, I was amazed that the majority of the people sitting around the conference table were discussing the legitimacy of this boy's giftedness. At 14 years old, Jeff already had quite a school history, which, truth be told, fizzled more than it sparkled. With an IQ of 145, but grades of D's and F's, Jeff was a walking frustration to most adults. The teachers' conversation went something like this:

"You know, if Jeff was really gifted, he'd show it once in a while."

"Yes, and his homework is never done . . ."

"And let's not even talk about his organizational skills! You know, the ones he doesn't have?"

I could tell that Jeff's mom wanted to interrupt and offer a different perspective—the one that noticed Jeff could read a 350-page historical novel in 2 days; or that he started his school career at age 5 with panache, vigor, and an urge to learn; or that Jeff's vocabulary and thinking processes were more advanced than that of most adults, including some of his teachers. Yet, she stayed mute. Why? She had expressed such realities before, only to be told that Jeff couldn't possibly be gifted with such low grades.

"Mrs. Rogers," the school counselor concluded, "I believe it is in Jeff's best interests to be moved out of the honors level classes. Perhaps he is too stressed by their rigor."

"Or not?" I added, daring to ask a question. "When does Jeff excel?"

This came as a jolt to many of Jeff's teachers. They had come to see this young man as lazy, disheveled, and obstinate; yet the few times Jeff did shine were when he was allowed to do projects of personal interest or open-ended assignments with multiple right answers—or no right answers at all. He loved logic puzzles and finished them quickly. He contributed to debates about politics or ecology or justice with a sense of sophistication and insight seldom observed in overzealous teens who often boast opinions without regard for the facts. In my mind, there was no doubting Jeff's giftedness. He simply chose not to display it in school activities that required him to do little more than regurgitate facts he had already learned years before. Jeff's teachers may have been disappointed in him, but the reverse was also true: Jeff was disappointed in them.

Perhaps this scenario is familiar to you, as Jeff may be a prototype for your own gifted sons or daughters who play by their own rules, not the school's. Or, you may be a parent who is thinking, "I guess I'm lucky that my child has always prized achievement." Whatever the case may be, know this: Giftedness should not—indeed, *must* not—be linked to achievement in order to be a legitimate entity. Calling Jeff (or anyone) gifted only when he can prove it by jumping through the artificial achievement hoops we place before him is equivalent to saying that a disease can only exist if its symptoms are obvious and visible.

As a parent, you may believe this already, as you have an asset that most schoolteachers do not: You have known your child from the start. Teachers, even the ones who work with our kids for several years, still see only a snapshot of students' full selves—a place-in-time moment that may or may not be an accurate depiction of the fullness of the child's being. It is your long-range opinion that matters most, and the key to getting others to see the giftedness in your child as being an inherent quality rather than a report card filled with A's is knowing, first and foremost, that your impressions are accurate.

As a parent . . . you have an asset that most schoolteachers
do not: You have known your child from the start.

Speaking of First Impressions . . .

My journey into the world of gifted children began in an odd
place: an elementary classroom for children identified with behavioral
disorders and/or learning disabilities. I was a freshly minted teacher
with a Master's degree in special education, and, like all freshly minted
teachers, I was going to rock the worlds of my students. They would
love school, respect themselves and me, and their learning curves
would always trend upward.

And then I met Matt. From day one, he was obstinate and angry.
His mom (his dad was absent) had moved him to yet another town
and yet another school—three schools in 6 years, in fact. He came
into my classroom with a scowl, plopped himself down at a desk apart
from any of his classmates, and leafed through the assignments I had
prepared carefully for him. The ones that met Matt's approval—the
challenging or creative ones—were done swiftly and accurately, but
any assignment that Matt found unworthy was promptly bunched into
a ball and thrown to my desk—a paper projectile on which Matt had
scribbled one word in red crayon: "irrelevant."

My ideals stayed in place for a while as I worked with Matt, convinced that at some point he would acquiesce to my teaching prowess
and complete the work I found to be important for him. That never
happened. Day after day, and then month after month, his "irrelevant"
paper bombs exploded onto my desk. No amount of praise, punishment, or ignoring changed this situation. This freshly minted teacher
was at his wit's end, his bag of instructional tricks as empty as a politician's promise.

And then something unexpected happened: Matt got sprayed by
a skunk before school one morning and entered our building with a
scent that could neither be ignored nor appreciated. Yet for the first
time, Matt's demeanor changed. He was smiling and talkative, sharing

how this smelly incident took place in his backyard, where he was checking on the sugar maple trees he had tapped to gather their sap and, with great time and effort, turn that sap into maple syrup. Having exhausted all other reasonable options, I cautiously made a suggestion to Matt: What if I changed his curriculum so that every school subject dealt with some aspect of maple sugar farming? Math could involve measurement and making change. Science could include lessons on how to make his product pure enough to sell at our one local grocery store (a community mentor helped with this), and social studies could involve a photo essay, complete with a script, on how to transform sap into syrup.

Matt took my bait, and from that day forward I never received another "irrelevant" wad of paper on my desk.

During that school year and the next, I saw something I didn't know was possible: a special education student on an Individual Education Plan (IEP) who also possessed tremendous academic and intellectual abilities. I needed to learn more, so I left my teaching position to begin a Ph.D. program focused on gifted children. To this day, I thank Matt—and that skunk—for altering my career focus permanently.

At the onset of my doctoral studies, I was fortunate to encounter two women whose views on giftedness mirrored my own nascent observation: that giftedness is not *something you do*, but rather *someone you are*. The best way to describe this distinction is to introduce you to both of these pioneers in the field of gifted education.

The first, Leta S. Hollingworth, is a woman I met only through her work. Hollingworth died in 1939, yet her work spoke to me in such a way that whenever I opened one of her books, I felt like we were sitting in a coffee shop in overstuffed chairs with worn upholstery—I, taking notes, and Leta, just talking. A school psychologist by trade, Hollingworth taught a course at Columbia University in 1916 on the psychology of children with limited intellectual capacity. Using the newly developed Stanford-Binet IQ test, Hollingworth wanted her students to see a contrast between children who scored at the lower limits of the test and one child who scored much higher. She arranged to test an 8-year-old boy called Child E, "who exhausted the scale without being fully measured by it, achieving an IQ of *at least* 187" (Hollingworth, 1942, p. xii). From this moment on, Hollingworth was hooked:

> I had tested thousands of incompetent persons, a majority of them children . . . this thoroughgoing experience of the negative aspects of intelligence rendered the performance of E even more impressive to me than it would otherwise have been. I perceived the clear and flawless working of his mind against a contrasting background of thousands of dull and foolish minds. It was an unforgettable observation. (p. xii)

Hollingworth did groundbreaking work in establishing the field of giftedness as a legitimate entity. In addition to being a psychologist and author, she also taught highly gifted children in a program she developed for the New York City public school system. In every regard, she came to see giftedness as a quality that can be measured at a young age and as a lifelong phenomenon that may or may not express itself in high achievement. Hollingworth's book, *Children Above 180 IQ Stanford-Binet*, published posthumously in 1942, contains many passages that, sadly, are as true today as they were then:

> This element in our juvenile population, so significant and so rarely found, passes unrecognized at present through the public schools. We have not even commenced to evolve an education suitable for a child who at 9 or 10 years of age is able to think on a college level. The idea that such children exist at all is even laughed to scorn by teachers and principals who have a quarter of a century of "experience" behind them. These children have no way of making themselves known. They become known only to those educators who "believe in" mental tests. (p. 320)

Hollingworth was wise enough to understand that there is a distinction between two terms that we currently—and erroneously—consider synonyms: *talent* and *giftedness*. To her, to me, and I hope to you, the distinction between these two terms is a necessary and important one. Here's how I see them:

- *Talent* invokes the idea of demonstrable skills in a specific domain, like math or soccer or dance. High academic achievers exhibit many of their talents through the curriculum that is offered to them, and we often identify children with these attributes for inclusion in gifted programs.
- *Giftedness* is an innate ability to both detect and comprehend the world in complex ways that differ significantly from age-expected norms. High academic achievement may or may not be present, but a lack of academic success does not "disqualify" one from being seen as gifted.

As you will read throughout this book, the definition and identification of giftedness are continuing conundrums with virtually no consensus, even among noted professionals who have spent their careers investigating the gifted population. Still, if we return to the groundbreaking work of Hollingworth, and the profound respect she held for children who were either talented, gifted, or both, we see that her wisdom transcends time.

Other important elements for parents to consider include the issues Hollingworth associated with gifted children in the social and emotional realms. Among these areas of concerns, Hollingworth (1942) pointed out the following:

- *Play and friendship*, as gifted children prefer complicated games instead of frivolous, unstructured games.
- *Negativity toward authority figures*, as gifted children often try to correct adults whom they know are wrong about something, yet are reprimanded for doing so because it is seen as disrespectful. The result? Animosity toward these adults from the gifted child.
- *Using their intellects to take advantage of others*, which Hollingworth labels as "benign chicanery," in which gifted children cajole others to do their bidding for tasks they find distasteful. (Think Tom Sawyer and the whitewashed fence incident.)

Indeed, Hollingworth's extensive work with gifted children as a psychologist and as a teacher contributed to the remarkable insights she had on this population of kids. If the true definition of a visionary is someone whose work is even more legitimate in the generations that follow its creation, then Hollingworth fits the bill. A champion of gifted children as people who must be acknowledged and accommodated, Hollingworth remains a beacon of hope for today's gifted children and those who care about them.

The other woman whom I encountered during my first year in studying gifted children was Annemarie Roeper. Unlike Hollingworth, Annemarie entered my life in the real sense, and the friendship we shared for more than three decades is among my most cherished relationships.

Annemarie worked with gifted children and their families beginning in 1942, when she and her husband, George, opened a school in southeastern Michigan, The Roeper School, based on a philosophy of global interdependence and personal, emotional well-being. Their school had a rich foundation, as Annemarie's parents ran a boarding school in rural Germany with similar emphases—Marienau School, which still exists today. At Marienau School and The Roeper School, academic achievement is prized, but it is considered to be only one part of a child's education; art, culture, and a firm understanding of the importance of each person's existence are the other colors on life's palette that are essential if one is to become truly educated, truly human. From humble origins as a preschool housed in the top floor of the Roepers' home, The Roeper School now boasts an enrollment of more than 600 gifted and creative children from preschool through 12th grade. As two parents said about their child's experiences at Roeper, "My son can write a paper with 35 footnotes, and he also knows that everybody deserves his respect," and "There's no division between jocks and intellectuals. It's assumed everybody has a body and a mind" (Delisle, 2005, p. 41).

The contributions made by George and Annemarie Roeper concerning the appropriate education of gifted young minds could fill volumes. A retrospective analysis of their work (Delisle & Schultz, 2016) gave credit to the significant contributions they both made to the education and well-being of gifted children. Arguably, though, the most important piece of the "gifted puzzle" to emerge from her 60+ years as an educator of and advocate for gifted children was Annemarie Roeper's (2000) startlingly simple and precise conception of giftedness: "Giftedness is a greater awareness, a greater sensitivity, and a greater ability to understand and transform perceptions into intellectual and emotional experiences" (p. 33).

Go ahead: Think of the gifted child or adult who brought you to open this book in the first place. Now, reread Annemarie's conception of giftedness. I'd bet a large wager that her conception of giftedness is more closely aligned to what you see in the gifted individual(s) in your life than any definition pointing to a particular IQ number or achievement test percentile that school districts often use in their identification protocols. As I noted earlier, and as any parent of a gifted child knows, gifted youngsters come to our attention first and foremost because of the sophisticated ways they perceive the world around them. True, their vocabularies may be large and arrive early, and their abilities to connect seemingly disparate concepts seem ingrained from an early age, but it is their overall awareness of and sensitivity to the people and surroundings that inhabit their lives that distinguishes them from their age-peers. And this, my friends, is giftedness.

Upon her retirement as headmistress of the Roeper School in 1983, Annemarie moved with George to California, where she developed the Annemarie Roeper Model of Qualitative Assessment (QA). During this assessment process, Annemarie would interview parents of a gifted child and the gifted child him- or herself, and then followed up with a final discussion with the parents in which recommendations for schools and family interaction were offered. The core of this QA was the interview with the child, which could last up to 90 minutes. As expressed by Annemarie:

> The goal is not for children to show how much they know or how bright they are, but who they are. The information presents itself in a pure form, almost like a byproduct. This is sacred information and must never be misused. . . . The child may keep a distance, seem to be oblivious of the evaluator, or

get close, touch, talk trustingly, excitedly, or be eager to share. The secret is to further the flow of expression, when needed, without changing it. (Roeper, 2004, p. 33)

And, at the session's conclusion . . .

It is amazing for me to see how reluctant the children usually are to leave, even though I am old, cannot hear well, cannot get down on the floor with them, and do not have the latest toys. It is because they feel understood, recognized and accepted. (Roeper, 2004, p. 33)

Knowing that she would not be around forever to conduct her QAs with children, Annemarie trained multiple colleagues in her methods. One of those individuals, Anne Beneventi (2016), had this to say about the importance of the QA methodology:

The true gift of QA is allowing children to be their authentic selves and seeing their wholeness . . . I will forever be grateful to Annemarie for her relational, respectful method of searching below the surface to capture the essence of the individual. (p. 257)

George Roeper died in 1992, and Annemarie followed him in 2012, both of them leaving a legacy about how the world should perceive and understand gifted children. Never having had a relationship with any of my familial grandparents, I "adopted" George and Annemarie as surrogate "gifted grandparents," and they willingly accepted that role. What a lucky man I was to have them in my life.

In conclusion, when determining what giftedness looks like, it would serve us well to consider the contributions of Leta Hollingworth and George and Annemarie Roeper. Pioneers all, they have established giftedness as an entity that can be measured best through observation and the careful, tender analysis of the child's abilities to perceive the world from a viewpoint that is both sophisticated and complex.

Reality Sets In

As you might imagine, the views of giftedness expressed by Hollingworth and the Roepers are not the ones used by school districts or departments of education in qualifying children for gifted program services. Far from it. Instead, the "definitions" of giftedness they use are often little more than mathematical formulae that result in two piles of kids—the "ins" and the "outs."

The small part of me that is realistic understands the reasoning behind this process. Indeed, it would be difficult to conduct Annemarie Roeper's QA on every child brought to the attention of school personnel as possibly being gifted. Because of prohibitive time and costs, this procedure is relinquished in favor of group scores on aptitude and achievement tests.

To be fair, this is not a bad place to begin; test scores can tell us which children are excelling in relation to their age-mates. The problem comes when the test scores become the *only* way for a child to gain access to gifted program services. As we know, some children do not test well, whether due to nervousness, a language or cultural difference, or because the child would rather make an intricate design on the bubble sheet than answer "stupid questions on a stupid test." So, if we stop at the test scores, we may be doing two bad things: (1) not identifying gifted kids who deserve to be noticed, and (2) overidentifying high achievers as gifted when they are little more than . . . well, high achievers.

Here is what should happen: Once test scores are collected, school personnel should pass around to the teachers the list of students who scored in the top 5% of each grade level, on aptitude (IQ), achievement, or both. Then, teachers should ask one simple question, "Who is not on this list who deserves closer examination?" Even if only a few names are suggested, these children can then be examined with a less numerically based procedure, perhaps one that approximates Roeper's QA or involves an examination of the child's body of work in or outside of school. Is this approach flawless? Hardly, because many teachers themselves see giftedness as synonymous with overall high academic achievement. Yet this simple procedure just might yield a bounty of gifted kids who may not qualify for the label by the more typical, number-based procedures. And honestly, if even one overlooked gifted child is located through this additional method, then time has been well spent.

If all else fails, and your child's school is reluctant (or worse) to look beyond the test scores, you may need to resort to an individual intellectual assessment conducted by the school's psychologist or a psychologist in private practice. This can be expensive, in terms of dollars and time, yet it is often worth the effort to have this test completed. Why? Because few school districts will discount the evaluation of a professional who is licensed to administer and interpret a noted IQ test like the Stanford-Binet or the Wechsler Intelligence Scale for Children (WISC).

Avoid at All Costs: The Definitional Quandary

Earlier, I made a distinction between *talent* and *giftedness*, the former being related to achievement-based outcomes, and the latter more focused on the entirety of a gifted child's being. Over the years, many heated debates have occurred between those who prefer one conception to the other. In fact, it's pretty safe to say that there are as many interpretations of talent and giftedness as there are people who have an opinion.

Lots of people and associations have attempted to define giftedness, including the federal government, which has a definition that blends elements that could satisfy both the "talent" and "gifted" camps. Almost every U.S. state, too, has a definition of giftedness, many of which are derivatives of the federal definition. Joseph Renzulli (1978), a pioneer in the field of gifted child education, developed the Three-Ring Conception of Giftedness, which is an admixture of advanced academic abilities, creativity, and motivation (which he called "task commitment"). The Columbus Group, composed of psychologists, educators, and advocates of giftedness from a variety of backgrounds, wrote a definition in 1991 that focused on the asynchrony that often exists between a gifted child's chronological age and his or her cognitive and emotional intensities (Morelock, 1992). Others, like Abraham Tannenbaum (1983), composed definitions of giftedness that include the element of chance (i.e., depending on when and where you are born, your gifts might or might not be recognized), while François Gagné (2004) used the terms *aptitudes* and *gifts* synonymously, and contended that young children have "undifferentiated" gifts that get more specialized as they mature. Too, there is Howard Gardner's (1983) idea of multiple intelligences, which appears to spread the quality of giftedness to just about everyone. Finally, the National Association for Gifted Children (2010) has had multiple definitions over the years, the most recent one being a monstrosity of confusing terms that is 224 words long and focuses almost entirely on domain-specific areas, like academics or the arts. And just in case 224 words isn't enough, this convoluted definition is followed by additional appendices, which add even more verbiage to the mix. One mother, commenting on her son's reaction to the equating of achievement with giftedness, crystalized his thoughts thusly:

> When my son discovered that some people equated giftedness with excelling in a specific domain, he became quite upset, wondering how it was that anyone who is supposed to know about giftedness would hold such a limited view. He said that giftedness to him is how he understands the world, how deeply he views things—neither of which is measurable by taking a test, getting straight A's or winning a prize. He said that's always been his problem—teachers want him to get straight A's rather then engage in a dialog about how he interprets literature or an event in history. What happens now with this NAGC definition? Will my son be found "not gifted" because his gifts lie in areas outside of specific domains? (personal communication, May 22, 2012)

Confused? I am, too. With so many smart people coming up with such diverse interpretations of giftedness, we probably look pretty foolish as a field of study to legislators and the general public who can't even get a straight answer to the question "So . . . what *exactly* is giftedness?" My advice on this definitional issue is this: Approach school personnel with questions about how *they* define and identify giftedness. A school's principal may or may not know this, but a gifted coordinator or school psychologist should. Once you find your answer, ask how this definition corresponds with methods of identifying gifted children in the district. So, if the district definition mentions "high potential," but the identification procedures only consider children with straight A's . . . then there is a mismatch. Pointing out this discrimination may not make you popular, but it does make you right. Indeed, no child with high aptitude should be denied gifted services due to a less-than-perfect report card.

Just as in politics, most of what is important in education is local. So, do your homework, find whatever information exists in your district about the identification and education of gifted children, and present your case like a well-prepared attorney. You will be taken more seriously if you have your facts in order.

Just a Word on Leveling: Giftedness Ain't Unitary

Most high schools offer a variety of sports venues, including intramurals, junior varsity, and varsity teams. Where you play depends on a number of factors—inherent ability, dedication to excellence, and the amount of time you are willing to commit to practice and drills. A kid who just wants to mess around and have fun with friends may find the intramural volleyball team to be a great option, while a budding Olympian may accept nothing more than top performance on the varsity swim team. And in the middle, you've got junior varsity (JV) squads, for kids who are serious about sports but not necessarily addicted to them. This diversity of athletic options makes sense, and it's replicated in orchestras and choruses, where the best violinists become first chair and the most accomplished singers get to do solo performances.

When I entered the field of gifted child education, I assumed the same distinctions would apply, and that there would be leveled services for gifted kids, depending on how gifted they actually were, because the reality is, some children are "JV gifted," and others are "varsity gifted" in ways that amaze the adults around them. I soon learned, though, that few school districts take the time to differentiate between levels of giftedness the same way that they do for athletes or musicians. Instead, all of the gifted kids are clustered under one label, often receiving the same services in the same classroom. Yet, even if IQ alone were used to identify these children, the range of scores might be from 130–180+, which is a far greater ability range than most coaches or maestros ever have to deal with on the same team or in the same orchestra.

Although it is hard to generalize about the needs of children I have not met, my experiences with gifted children lead me to state the following:

- Children with IQs in the 130–140 range can often be accommodated in regular classrooms where teachers adjust the curriculum to meet their advanced abilities. Social and emotional difficulties are uncommon, as there is a large enough pool of children with similar abilities that legitimate friendships can be formed.
- Children with IQs in the 140–160 range can seldom be accommodated sufficiently in an educational environment that merely "stretches" or enriches the curriculum. Intensive modification of curriculum, including grade-skipping, needs to be considered as viable. Too, age-mates may offer little social sustenance, as these children will prefer—and need— the company of older, intelligent children and/or adults.
- Children with IQs above 160 have academic, intellectual, and social and emotional needs that are so unique that typical school resources will be unable to provide fully for their education. For these rare children, a team of professionals (including a teacher, gifted expert, parents, and a psycholo-

gist) will need to be convened, much as a similar team would be gathered for a child with severe learning difficulties. These profoundly gifted children are more at risk than others if their level of giftedness is not addressed directly.

In recent years, more information and resources have become available for highly gifted children and their parents, including such prominent and necessary organizations as the Davidson Institute for Talent Development, the Institute for Educational Advancement, and Supporting Emotional Needs of the Gifted (SENG; see the Resources section for information on these and other resources). Just know this: Because giftedness varies in both depth and range, your advocacy efforts on behalf of your child will need to take into account both of these realities—*depth* and *range.* If "one-size-fits-all" isn't true for shoes, shirts, or varsity football teams, then it is equally unrealistic to believe that a single gifted program can serve the needs of its many unique members.

Talking the Talk

A wise 14-year-old girl, highly gifted and highly verbal, once asked me the following questions: "Have you watched adults squirm and listened to their responses when you ask them if they're gifted? What does this say about how they define giftedness, and what messages does this send to people, especially kids, about giftedness being okay?"

Even though most parents see giftedness as a positive attribute, they are often reluctant to talk openly about the term and its implications with their children. Fearing their gifted children will become "elitist" or "big-headed" if the term is discussed, parents downplay the term and advise their gifted children to do the same, "so that other kids don't feel bad."

Yeah . . . just like you'd be quiet about it if your child happened to be a star athlete!

By not discussing giftedness, or by telling your gifted child to avoid mention of it around others, you are sending a confusing mixed message: *Be proud of your abilities, but don't let anyone know that you have them.*

An attitude of humility regarding one's advanced abilities is understandable, but it can go too far. When it gets to the point where a gifted child appears downright embarrassed to say that he is in a gifted program, or that he has skipped a grade because of his strong academic abilities, the child is not being humble, but dishonest. So are you, if you promote such behavior.

When your child is identified as gifted, take time to sit down with him or her and explain *in your own words* what you think this term means. Give your child some cues that you picked up when she was at an early age ("You know, Shawna, I remember you were reading cereal boxes and road signs when you were not even 2 years old."), and let her know that just because she may learn quicker than other kids, that doesn't imply an inherent superiority as a human being. Your child might be *better at* many things than the kid next door, but that does not mean that he or she is *better than* that child in any way. Next, ask your gifted children if they ever noticed that they can do things or understand things that many kids their age do not yet get. And, ask them if they often find that they like talking or playing with older kids or adults, as the level of understanding or camaraderie in these mixed-age groupings just seems like a comfortable, intellectual fit. If they say they do like the company of elders, tell them that this is common among gifted kids.

By not discussing giftedness, or by telling your gifted child to avoid mention of it around others, you are sending a confusing mixed message: *Be proud of your abilities, but don't let anyone know that you have them.*

Next, be ready for the inevitable question, "Mom (Dad) . . . were you gifted?" First, you will chuckle, as kids always ask this question in the past tense, as if your own giftedness as a parent somehow went away or awry in the adult years. Follow your guffaw with a genuine answer that doesn't fall back on the standard nonresponse of "We didn't have gifted programs when I was in school." Your children are not asking whether you were placed in gifted classes. They are asking, "Are you like me?" Be honest with a genuine "yes" or "no," as it can open the door up to a conversation about a word that needs to be taken out of the closet and shaken from its musty, stale image: *gifted*.

Another thing: When your child comes home with the tears flowing after a bad day at school (it'll happen) because someone made fun of "a gifted kid" getting a low grade on some meaningless test, she'll probably ask you this: "Why do I have to be gifted? Why can't I just be normal like everyone else?" You need to be prepared. The word *normal* is a loaded word, as its opposite, *abnormal*, is something few of us aspire to be. Contrasting the terms *gifted* and *normal* implies that giftedness is an aberration, a flaw, something to be avoided. Hear your child out, and then ask her to substitute only one word—change *normal* to *typical*. The plaintive cry of "Why can't I be typical?" sounds just a bit less harsh, doesn't it? With a little cajoling and a dose of hot cocoa, you might even get into a discussion of how giftedness is often determined by a child's ability to do things before most other kids can. It may be atypical to know your alphabet by 18 months, but because all kids learn the alphabet in their own time, there's nothing abnormal about that, is there?

One last thing you need to be ready to address, not directly with your gifted children but with some of the adults around them, is this: Neighbors, family members, and even some school personnel might say something to you like, "I *hate* the fact that we have gifted programs at all. Everyone is gifted in some way, right? Also, putting some kids in gifted classes while excluding others just makes the nonincluded kids feel bad." When you hear comments like these, the first thing to do is ignore your natural instincts to attack the person's biased ignorance. Instead, a polite (but pointed) response is called for. Something like this: "Actually, not everyone is gifted in some way, just as not everyone is athletic or musical or mathematically precocious. Yes, each child is a unique and special individual, but not every one of them is gifted."

Then, you can address Part 2 of this person's comment: "And, as far as not offering gifted classes and opportunities to kids who need them, remember that no one has the moral right to hold one child back to make another child feel better." This sentiment, which is attributed to gifted advocate Stephanie Tolan, might convince even the seemingly inconvincible that gifted services are essential, not tangential.

After that, walk away and find some more astute discussants.

In the next chapter, we'll take a closer look at that distinction between *better at* and *better than*, especially as it might impact social relationships. For now, though, I leave you with some wise words that might spur even more discussion with your children about the meaning of this often misunderstood term, *gifted*.

Gifted Children Speak Out

"The best part of being gifted is that I get to hold intelligent conversations with intelligent people. Also, I have enough intelligence to control my life and where I want to go with it. The worst part? Discrimination: My abilities are held against me."

—Girl, 14, Sydney, Australia

"There have been several times when I won't tell people about my gifted school or me being classified as gifted. The reason is when other kids hear my school's name, the first thing they say is, 'He thinks he's better than we are.' Actually, it's just the opposite: I just want to be a kid and just be me."

—Boy, 16, Ohio

"Sometimes, when I'm trying to fit in and have fun, I don't want to show people my differences. I don't push the fact that I'm gifted in other people's faces. That would just turn them off. I usually appear the same as them and wait for them to discover on their own that I might have a gift."

—Girl, 14, Maine

Chapter 2

Know the Distinction Between "Better at" and "Better Than"

I've gotta be honest: Those first two years of teaching in northern New Hampshire, where I met Matt, my "maple sugar kid," taught me more about teaching gifted kids than a new teacher of children with disabilities could ever have expected. Here's another example as to how: There were only three conditions under which we would not have outdoor recess—if the temperature was lower than -10° F, if there was a moose in the schoolyard (yes, it happened), or if the town drunk, Mr. Shibley, was on the swings again. Barring these circumstances . . . out we went! And, it was during one of my daily recess duties that I first came to learn of the plight of gifted children when it comes to honest communication.

Two first-grade boys were having a fight. No blood or weapons were involved, just a lot of screaming and flailing of little arms that never hit their intended targets. As I calmed the boys down, one of the young combatants hurled off some verbal insults to his opponent: "I hate you! You're stupid! You're a pig!" Not to be outshouted, the other boy—who I knew from reputation to be very bright—spouted off the ultimate degradation, "I might be a pig, but you're a Neanderthal!"

The world stopped for a moment, as the young audience who had gathered looked at one another with wrinkled noses and sighed a collective "Huh?" Imagine—being so smart that even your insults are misunderstood.

Don't get me wrong, I'm not in favor of anything that hints of an insult or put-down, yet I do suspect that when such negative verbiage is spewed, the spewer intends for the spewee to comprehend it. After all, how can we call it communication if the message sent is never truly received?

The distinction between *better at* and *better than* involves many issues that serve gifted children well, if they understand what they are. Too often called *nerd*, *geek*, *smarty pants*, *brainiac*, or worse, gifted kids need to know that the source of these insults is one of two things— envy or ignorance. However, when a gifted kid tries to defend himself from name calling by telling his accuser, "You're only saying that because you're jealous of my abilities," or "If you weren't so stupid you'd get what I'm saying," well, it doesn't improve the situation.

Let's delve into this fine-line distinction by returning to the work of someone you've already met, Leta Hollingworth.

On Suffering Fools Gladly

A lesson which many gifted persons never learn as long as they live is that human beings in general are inherently very different from themselves in thought, in action, in general intention, and in interests. Many a reformer has died at the hands of a mob that he was trying to improve in the belief that other human beings can and should enjoy what he enjoys. This is one of the most painful and difficult lessons that each gifted child must learn, if personal development is to proceed successfully. It is more necessary that this be learned than that any school subject be mastered. (Hollingworth, 1942, pp. 259–260)

The wisdom of Hollingworth's statements transcends time once again. Because no child rises after a full night's sleep, stretches to awaken tired muscles and brain cells, and states openly, "Gee . . . I wonder who I can get to hate me today at school," it is obvious that person-to-person communication is valued. No one seeks to be isolated or void of friendships and lunchtime buddies, but more than occasionally, gifted children find themselves spending time alone, at least intellectually. Barely keeping their heads above water in discussing topics of little interest to them, gifted kids often wonder, "Isn't there someone like *me* out there?"

It's at this point that you, as a parent, need to intervene and present two realities to your gifted child—the idea of suffering fools gladly, and, simultaneously, the distinction between age-mates and peers.

First, let's review *suffering fools gladly* through a fairly common example. A bunch of 5-year-olds get together and decide to play a game. One of them, your gifted daughter, can't wait to play; games have rules, people take turns, and there is a goal to achieve, like being the first player to enter Candy Land. Before the game even starts, though, there are squabbles—two kids fight over who gets the blue marker, no one seems to get that all people play first before your turn comes around again—indeed, the idea of taking turns just seems foreign to your daughter's playmates. So, she responds by taking charge, assigning roles, and saying things like "It's not your turn yet." The other kids look at her as the spoilsport, saying she is no fun and a bad friend. In essence, your daughter's intellect and maturity cause her to define *fun* differently than do most 5-year-olds. Whereas your gifted daughter's idea of fun is playing games by established rules that result in winners and losers, her 5-year-old age-mates—not peers—are simply content with messing around aimlessly until the next playtime distraction presents itself. In the end, the other kids walk away, leaving your daughter sad, disillusioned, and confused.

Fast-forward 10 years, to that level of hell Dante forgot to write about in *The Divine Comedy*—ninth grade. Your gifted son is excited that the enthusiastic student teacher has selected *Romeo and Juliet* as the class reading assignment. It won't be a watered-down version translated into modern English; it will be the original play—just as

Shakespeare wrote it. There will even be a chance to act out some of the scenes, with classmates playing the roles of the main characters. Then it happens: Between some kids saying, "This stuff makes no sense," to others giggling over the thought that their classmates might touch hands—or kiss!—if they play their roles as written, the serious intent of the student teacher is DOA. Your son comes home, slams his books on the kitchen table, and shouts (as if it's your fault), "Why can't these kids GROW UP? I'm SICK of them!"

These two scenes, if they occur repeatedly throughout the lives of gifted children, could cause them to resent the people with whom they spend many of their days—their classmates. In a valiant effort to get other children to comprehend and appreciate the bigger picture, gifted kids become the know-it-alls, the too-smart-for-their-own-good geeks who only want things their way. No longer willing to agonize silently, these socially maligned gifted children may lash out—somewhere, sometime—or even worse, repress their feelings, causing a turmoil that cripples their insides.

That's why the notion of suffering fools gladly needs to be raised as soon as you witness an incident like this. Tell your child the truth: "The kids who don't want to play games by the rules or have no idea of the relevance of Shakespeare *are* immature by comparison to you. However, they are not being immature on purpose. Right now, this is simply who they are."

Such a statement may not bring a lot of solace to your child, but it presents him or her with a stark reality that he or she may, indeed, encounter into adulthood—age and maturity are sometimes poles apart. Also, gifted children need to know that trying to convince classmates (or, in the future, colleagues) that they are acting more like their hat sizes than their ages will not be met with a lot of favorable responses, for just as you don't understand your classmates or colleagues, at times they just don't get you either. Hollingworth's advice? If you try to reform the mob, you may be the one who is martyred.

So, what to do? Here's where you bring out the heavy social artillery—reviewing the distinction between age-mates and peers. Simply put, an age-mate is someone who was born in (or close to) the same year as you. You may or may not have a lot in common other than the proximity of your birthdays, but the assumption is that you are peers because of this similarity in chronology. For reasons that have more to do with convenience than research evidence, schools are established around the age-mate concept, as the vast majority of kids start kindergarten at age 5 and graduate high school at 18. So, in reality, class placement is determined by age, not by readiness to learn. There may be some exceptions to this age-based rule, especially in high schools, but for the most part, kids are clustered with their age-mates for the majority of their school experiences, based on the assumption that there is no need to stray too far from chronological compatriots to find social and intellectual satisfaction. Like many assumptions about gifted children, this idea is misguided, but that seldom matters to the place keepers, who want to group kids together solely because they are all 5 or 10 or 14 years old.

If you find that your gifted children want to hang out more with you, a grandparent, or an older sibling than chronological age-mates, the reason is obvious: There's no need to explain who they are or how they know what they know.

A peer, by contrast, is someone who shares your passions, your humor, and your drive. You can talk for hours about anything—or nothing at all—and there is a sense of comfort present that you can say what you want, even using that big vocabulary that makes your age-mates twitch their noses in confusion. How old you are is either irrelevant or of minor importance, and is generally only raised as an issue by someone who does not understand that soul mates seldom factor in age as a variable for friendship.

So, if you find that your gifted children want to hang out more with you, a grandparent, or an older sibling than chronological age-mates, the reason is obvious: There's no need to explain who they are or how they know what they know. When children are accepted as bright, competent individuals, the stigma of being smart is no longer a stigma at all.

Ironically, this age-mate/peer distinction seems both understood and accepted once K–12 schooling is complete. When you are in college or employed, people of all ages study, work, and play together, and I have yet to see a party invitation for adults include the notation, "Sorry, if you are younger than 25 or older than 32, please pass along this invitation to someone who is within that age bracket." Let your gifted child know this, too: As years pass, their specific age will play less and less of a factor in socialization. This is not to say that they won't meet some grown-ups who remain the dolts they were in high school, but it does open up the social arena to a whole batch of people who may have been off limits during the K–12 years. Try as we might, as parents, to change everything negative for our children into something positive, that's not always possible. A simple statement—"Just hang on . . . things will get better in time"—is an honest declaration of the inconvenient social reality that many gifted kids encounter in their early years.

There is, though, one group of age-mates who can also play the role of peers: other gifted children. Time and again, you will hear gifted children say that they appreciate their advanced classes for two reasons—the education they are receiving and the people who surround them in learning it. Indeed, I would argue that the greatest benefit of gifted programming is not the high-level content the students study, but the benefit of learning alongside "like minds." You know, those kids who, in a schoolyard fight among first graders, would understand the word *Neanderthal* . . . and might even know its correct pronunciation.

Oh! The Silly Things We Do!

I was sharing a morning with 50 gifted middle school students in rural Montana (I know . . . that's redundant). We were having wide-ranging discussions on all things gifted, and when the topic of career options arose, students mentioned the usual collection of gifted-sounding professions they'd like to pursue—medicine, law, engineering—while a good number of them said (wisely, from my perspective), "I have no idea." But one girl, Maya, was fully animated as she described her career of choice: a makeup artist for zombie movies. Dressed all in black with eye makeup and lipstick to match, Maya had obviously embraced her career-calling personally.

A few minutes later, during a break in our discussions, I approached this young lady and asked her to tell me more about her career choice. She eyed me suspiciously, uttering one word with an arched eyebrow: "Seriously?"

"Yeah, " I responded, "I love zombie movies, especially *Shaun of the Dead*, and I always wondered how much time and talent it takes to make living people look dead."

For the remainder of our break time, Maya described how much science and creativity is needed to achieve the desired "dead effect," and she elaborated on particular makeup artists whose work she admired. When our conversation ended, I thanked Maya for her input. A few seconds later, she responded with her own thank-you: "You know," she said, "no adult has ever asked me why I wanted to be a makeup artist. Thank you for listening to me. It may not be as important a career as being a doctor, but it fits who I am."

I have no idea if Maya will keep or change her career direction in the future, but what is important is this: At least one adult in her life, other than a passing-through consultant, needs to take her dream seriously, not jokingly. Telling her that she is "wasting her gifts" by choosing to do makeup is a comment that erases the dreams of a bright adolescent who is just starting to realize her own individuality. Yet when it comes to gifted kids, otherwise-smart adults do this all of the time: They discount the importance of simply listening to a child's goals and asking why they are so important to that child.

The same thing is true in many other arenas of raising a gifted child. For example, when we mention how surprised we are when a gifted child does something silly or wrong ("I expected more common sense from a smart girl like you!"), we are actually setting the scene for social and emotional trouble, because, intended or not, such a statement conveys our belief that gifted kids are paragons of perfection. Here are some other silly ways adults put gifted students on edge and at risk for social isolation and emotional discomfort:

- *Forgetting that they are children first and gifted second.* Often, gifted children act more responsibly than other kids their age. They remember their school assignments and household chores, and if we ask them to remind us of an important date, deadline, or appointment, they'll often do so. Conversations with adults are likely to be appropriate, and the use of logic instead of tantrums is generally how conflicts at school or in the family are resolved. And then, there are the days when *none* of these things is true and you begin to wonder if that gifted child you saw yesterday had an overnight lobotomy. Scratching your head, you say to yourself, "I thought he was smarter than this." The thing is, kids are supposed to be immature, selfish, forgetful, and less concerned about tomorrow than today. That's their job. Just because gifted children tend to act this way less often than others their age does not mean we should chide them when they do act their age. So, cut your gifted kids some slack: When they act their age, try to remember that being gifted is a *part* of who they are, but it is not their entire identity. Sometimes, they just want to be silly or immature. As do their parents.

The thing is, kids are supposed to be immature, selfish, forgetful, and less concerned about tomorrow than today. That's their job. Just because gifted children tend to act this way less often than others their age does not mean we should chide them when they do act their age.

- *Putting the gifted child on display for other adults.* We are proud of our children for many reasons—their kindness, their accomplishments, their desire to learn all they can from anyone they can. However, there are times when parents take this pride too far. Here's an example: "Honey, when company comes over tonight, will you play your violin for them? I'm sure they'd love to hear you!" Some kids will *relish* this chance to perform in front of others, but then there are whose who, through gritted teeth, may comply grudgingly or may decide to play in such an off-key way that the cat seeks cover. If this happens, your company will squirm as if sitting on rocks—and, when it's over, your child will have succeeded: She'll never again be asked to perform in the living room. So, be cautious of such public displays of your gifted child's private talents. If she chooses to perform in a school orchestra—no problem. And if your company goes to such a musical performance—hey, in that case, your child knows what she's getting into. But performing at home when the child's preference would be to greet your company politely and then exit for a round of reading or video games is not a way to build pride; it is, for you, a way to boast.

- *Putting the gifted child on display in front of other kids.* Again, if it's a band concert, a soccer match, a spelling bee, or a stage production of *Our Town*, observers expect to be wowed. Kids and adults alike realize that in a competitive event or in a culminating show based on much practice, the best that you can be is . . . the best! However, if a teacher singles out a student in class by saying, "There was only one A on Friday's test. Can anyone guess who got it?" or "I wish *all* of you would follow Felipe's lead and read books that are longer than 100 pages," the comment itself may be having the exact opposite of the intended effect. For smart kids, it doesn't take them long to realize that to avoid this unwanted adulation in front of class mates, all they have to do is give wrong answers on purpose, pick shorter books from the library, or leave their hands down in class even when they know the right answer to the teacher's question. Game playing? You bet. But, in the world of social survival, it's a game worth winning if you are a gifted kid who doesn't want to stand out at the cost of social acceptance. We can never forget that our gifted kids are still a part of a larger social milieu in which they have to play multiple roles—sometimes as the "smart kids," and sometimes as the bystanders who let other kids' talents shine above their own.

- *Expecting gifted children to be natural leaders.* Some gifted children love the limelight and seek it out whenever and however they can. Extroverted by nature, these confident children have Teflon personalities that ward off criticisms from age-mates and adults whose expectations of their leadership abilities are far too low. Then there are those gifted children who are quieter, more reserved, less prone to seek recognition than to amble through life undetected, seldom drawing attention to themselves or their accomplishments. Neither of these types of children is right or wrong, good or bad—the differences are simply innate, a quirk in individual personalities that makes the entire human race so interesting. However, there is a myth that pervades the gifted community: that *all* gifted children are our future leaders and, as such, they should start preparing for these destiny-driven roles right now. Indeed, gifted programs are sometimes defended by zealots who proclaim that if we don't address the needs of gifted kids today, we are tossing aside tomorrow's change makers by ignoring them.

  Well, not exactly. Although many of our gifted children will grow to become tomorrow's societal mucky-mucks, some of them won't, by either choice or default. Further, there will be children who have never been identified as gifted who will rise to levels of prominence few teachers would have predicted. We just don't know who will be what, do we? So, to state unequivocally that gifted children will grow to become our future leaders is an insult to one group (those nongifted kids who may grow up to surprise us with their talents) and a source of intense, unwanted pressure on those young people who wear the gifted tag. Should we encourage our gifted kids to use their talents on behalf of others? Of course! But should we demand it of them? My answer is "no."

Loneliness and Being Alone: A Fine-Line Distinction

Currently, I teach part-time in a public high school for highly gifted students in South Carolina. When they enter ninth grade, they also enter college, as they begin taking university courses along with high school Advanced Placement (AP) and honors-level classes. By high school graduation, most students have accumulated more than 70 college credits—all for free. Yeah, it's an awesome school.

Because the student body is just shy of 200, everyone pretty much knows one another, which is, of course, both a blessing and a curse. Personal relationships develop quickly—that's the blessing—but with so few students in attendance, the inevitable high school drama is accentuated, and social situations can get dicey at times. When this occurs, some students just want to escape into their own spaces.

Consider Peyton: Typically vibrant and talkative in class, Peyton disappears when lunchtime arrives. She ambles into a private study carrel or, weather permitting, goes outside and finds a tree whose shade she enjoys. Sometimes she has a book, but most times not. Instead, she just sits alone, enveloped in her personal thoughts, comfortable with the quiet that surrounds her. I caught her attention one day as lunch period ended. She had an exquisite sense of calm pervading her whole body and, without even being prompted to say anything, Peyton looked at me and said, "Lunch is always so refreshing." Comfortable around her classmates, Peyton is also comfortable by herself, a blend of being a social butterfly and a selective social orphan.

I use Peyton's example because one of any parent's greatest fears—whether or not his or her child is gifted—is that the child will be lonely, friendless, and separated from the social milieu that turns loners into isolates. The entire world is a social fabric of interactions with others, and if we find that our children are left out of the weave, we fear for them, and rightly so.

For reasons already explained in this chapter, gifted children may appear to be more timid in social situations where they perceive themselves as outsiders looking in. However, be reassured that gifted children generally seek the same type of social comforts others enjoy and that they seldom make active attempts to be antisocial. Still, being alert to Hollingworth's (1942) wise assertion that isolation is the "refuge of genius, not its goal," parents of gifted children do want to be vigilant toward their child's interactions, or lack thereof, with classmates, age-mates, and peers. But, as Peyton's case demonstrates clearly, these interactions might be accompanied by something euphemistically called *alone time*, an essential element in the life of many a gifted individual.

Being *alone* means that you value your mind enough that you would like it to accompany you occasionally on an otherwise solo mission into better understanding yourself and the world.

There is a difference between being lonely and simply being alone. Being *lonely* hurts, and it is a state often accompanied by sadness, resignation, or lethargy. Being *alone* means that you value your mind enough that you would like it to accompany you occasionally on an otherwise solo mission into better understanding yourself and the world. Through generations of work with gifted individuals, it has been found that this alone time is often a necessary and valuable adjunct to one's more social interactions. A mind whirring with ideas, insights, and possibilities sometimes needs time to churn these things together in a cauldron of quiet reflection. This isolation is not to be dismissed as trivial, for as Peyton discovered, this alone time was her time to ponder the wonders of the universe, or to simply relax her ever-active brain for a few moments of peaceful reflection.

In closing this chapter, here's another story: I was working with a group of 20 highly gifted children at a weekend retreat for them and their parents at a tucked-away piece of heaven in the Sierra Nevadas. The children did not know each other before this weekend, and many of them, even at the tender ages of 4–10, had been burned by unfulfilling contacts with kids their own ages. Then, the activities began, discussions ensued, sandcastles were constructed, and meals were shared.

At the Sunday evening closing dinner, an unusually reserved 10-year-old boy had a personal message to leave with the assembled group: "I wasn't really sure I wanted to come here for this," Anthony explained, "but this has been the best weekend of my life."

Anthony, surrounded by others like himself in terms of interests and intellectual sophistication, found something in this gifted group that he had never found before—peers aplenty. Talk with your gifted kids about the distinction between loneliness and being alone, and allow them (and yourself) to be comfortable with the quiet times that rejuvenate their very active minds.

Gifted Children Speak Out

"Sometimes when I am helping another person by explaining a problem, they still don't get it and complain that I am too complicated. I don't understand why they don't get it, and my explaining how to get the answer makes it more complicated to them than the original problem."

—Boy, 10, Indiana

"Everyone has what they were born with. The most value is how much people help people, not how smart or pretty they are. Me thinking I'm better because I'm smart is just the same as someone thinking they're better because they are pretty."

—Girl, 12, Alaska

"Kids in my school are just like crabs in a bucket. They pull each other right back down."

—Boy, 14, Utah

Chapter 3

Stop Paying Interest on a Bill You Never Owed

L ife is filled with false alarms. Thinking you left the front door open or the iron plugged in, you rush home to find that everything is locked up and turned off. Or, your 7-year-old runs into the house screaming, "Mom! Mom! Come here! Quick!" In a frenzy of motion, you rush to aid your child, who excitedly shows you the blue shell of a robin's egg she found in the backyard. "Isn't it pretty?" your child beams, while you double-check your supply of antacids.

There are so many real sources of fear and foreboding in our world, that it is pointless to manufacture any more, yet we do it all of the time. The same is true when it comes to personality traits possessed by many gifted people. What should be seen as pieces of wonder, excitement, imagination, and insight are too often interpreted as weirdness, eccentricity, illogic, and illusionary realities. We take the qualities that cause a gifted person to see the world from a slightly different vantage than most, and we try to homogenize them into the more common, acceptable views of existence. Thus, fuchsia fades to pink. Goldenrod melts to yellow. Sapphire becomes dark blue.

There are lots of ways to describe the previous examples, but the "term du jour" that seems to have captured the attention of many folks in the gifted child education field is *intensities*. These intensities in your gifted child can take many forms, but instead of giving you a technical definition right away, let's simply consider what they look like in your home:

- Your son's teacher sends you a note that reads, "Although I love Joey's enthusiasm, he must stop shouting out his answers in class. Also, please talk to him about the incessant tapping of his pencil, and the need to sit down when he is doing his worksheets instead of disrupting the class with his constant pacing."
- You take your teenage daughter to an art museum and split up so each family member can visit his or her favorite galleries. An hour later, you find your daughter just where you left her, and there are tears in her eyes. "This single painting carries the essence of what it means to be human," she says. It's then that you realize she has spent her whole time gazing at this one piece of artwork.
- You are packing the last of the boxes on the moving van when you spy your 10-year-old carefully tearing a bit of wallpaper from the living room. Upon closer examination, you see that he has pieces of wallpaper from every room tucked away in a shoebox. "These will help me remember every room in the most special house in the world," he explains to you.
- After your 4-year-old falls in the driveway, scraping her knee, you take her in your arms to comfort her tears. Once soothed, she looks you straight in the eye and says, "Mommy, it's never going to get better than this."

Sadly, when many people who don't understand the needs or characteristics of gifted individuals confront these intensities in others (or themselves, for that matter), their first reaction is to want to tamp them down . . . to make them less volatile . . . to "normalize" these over-the-top reactions. Rather than cherish these intensities and the people who have them, folks who don't understand that these intensities are just a part of the gifted individual's DNA complain about how "messy" they make life for everyone involved. So, instead of talking with Joey's teacher about ways to channel his intellectual excitement, we come up with behavior charts and fake awards Joey earns if he sits for 20 minutes without getting up. Or, we chastise our daughter for missing out on the new Abyssinian exhibit because she just sat and stared at "a picture, a single, stupid picture" for an hour. We roll our eyes at the wallpaper incident, lecturing about the need not to damage property or take things that no longer belong to us. Finally, we tell our sensitive 4-year-old that she needs to be more careful in the driveway, effectively ignoring the power of her sentiment. In ways both subtle and all-too-obvious, society tries to transform these unique perceptions into commonplace, standard-issue behaviors, beliefs, perceptions, and attitudes. When this occurs, we chip away so much of the essence of giftedness that the block that remains is just a remnant of its former self. To tweak the metaphor of this chapter's title just a little more directly, by asking gifted children to "quiet down" their brains, emotions, and imaginations and to see things in more typical ways, we are telling them that the interest is due on their childhood notions and they must "pay up" by relinquishing these views in an effort to fit in with everyday notions of reality. In truth, though, they owe no bill at all. They are just being themselves.

By asking gifted children to "quiet down" their brains, emotions, and imaginations and to see things in more typical ways, we are telling them that the interest is due on their childhood notions and they must "pay up" by relinquishing these views in an effort to fit in with everyday notions of reality. In truth, though, they owe no bill at all. They are just being themselves.

The Wonderful Wizard of OEs

Many people have come to the rescue of intense gifted kids and tried to help others to understand that their powerful feelings, insights, and emotions are more typical than unusual in this population. Yet there is one person, above all others, who made the world a little more palatable for those individuals who experience life in a higher key: Michael Piechowski. Born in Poland, Piechowski immigrated to the United States to pursue two (not just one!) Ph.Ds.—the first in molecular biology and the second in counseling psychology. Indeed, who better to know about the inner workings of gifted individuals than someone who has studied them at both an emotional and a molecular level?

Piechowski came to know a psychiatrist named Kazimierz Dabrowski at his first academic appointment at the University of Alberta. Dabrowski had written extensively, in Polish, on people who experienced life in ways that were more intense and vivid than most. Some of these people Dabrowski studied had been diagnosed with mental illnesses and were perceived as psychoneurotic by physicians, who saw their behaviors and perceptions as erratic and odd. Hospitalization and medication were often prescribed to "cure" these individuals.

Dabrowski had another take on this; he did not see mental illness at all, but rather individuals who were suffering in a different way. As Piechowski recalled:

> Dabrowski felt a great urgency to help and save those who are sensitive, vulnerable, empathetic, and creative, but who are not well adapted to the world where aggressive competition pushes people to get ahead with little consideration for their fellow humans. (as cited in Delisle, 2005, p. 218)

Because Dabrowski's books had never been translated adequately into English, these two Polish dynamos met regularly to do exactly that: make Dabrowski's powerful thoughts and words more understandable to many. Eventually, Piechowski (1986) gleaned from his mentor the Theory of Positive Disintegration, a complex structure detailing how some humans systematically achieve areas of self-knowledge and self-actualization by "disintegrating" former, less "emotionally complicated" versions of themselves into newer, more complex iterations. Taking this theory and elaborating upon it with his own brand of realism, Piechowski coined the term *overexcitabilities* (OEs), which is a psychological umbrella encompassing several different domains of human interaction: psychomotor, sensual, intellectual, imaginational, and emotional. Thanks to Piechowski's work, the gifted person's seemingly bothersome intensities took on a new spin—a positive one.

The OEs in More Depth

In a personal conversation with me, Piechowski joked that the term *OE* can stand for two things—overexcitability or "original equipment," as the nature of these OEs is inborn in those who have them in abundance. Let's examine the five OEs in greater detail, with an eye toward helping our gifted children better understand and appreciate what they are and how they can be helpful.

Psychomotor Overexcitability

Psychomotor overexcitability is often characterized as a surplus of physical energy that can be seen in a variety of ways: rapid speech with marked excitement ("Ooh! Ooh! Teacher! Pick me! Pick me!"), intense physical activity in organized sports (or simply at recess), and impulsive actions or nervous habits, like nail biting or pencil drumming. Piechowski and Cunningham (1985) found that psychomotor overexcitability alone does not distinguish gifted children from average ones; however, when this physical energy combines with intense intellectual exploration, the result is often an out-of-his-seat whiz kid who grates on his teacher's last nerve. As you might imagine, a misdiagnosis of Attention Deficit/Hyperactivity Disorder (ADHD) is not uncommon for children (and adults) who show these overexcitable signs (Webb et al., 2016). However, the distinction between a true case of ADHD and the situation of a gifted person who is overexcitable in the psychomotor domain is that the OE individual is able to focus for extended time periods on topics of intellectual interest *even while in constant motion.* When their cognitive juices are flowing, the only ADHD thing about these students is that they tend to ignore the mundane distractions of everyday life (like the teacher reciting the night's homework assignment). In essence, the frequent physical movements that children with psychomotor OE exhibit *enhance* their learning rather than *distract* them from it. To be sure, others around them—kids and adults—may not see these movements in as positive a light, but to the psychomotor gifted child, this motion is directed toward improved learning.

Helping your child control these psychomotor impulses can be as difficult as herding cats in an open field, for movement is as natural to them as singing is to a contralto. Giving quieter options is one possibility, such as, "Frank, if you must drum with your pencil, hit your legs instead of your desk. The teacher won't hear it." Or, in the case of a child who blurts out in class, "Jen, when an answer comes into your mind, scribble it into your notebook, and I promise to get back to you about it later." However, as you might imagine, these gimmicks are temporary fixes, at best. The best solution is not a solution at all, but a situation—find teachers who tolerate movement and encourage it as just another way to learn. So, if your daughter fidgets while sitting at her desk during silent reading, what's the harm in having her stand, or lie down on the pillows in the back of the room, or sit in the rocking chair that most teachers who appreciate kids like this always seem to have in their classrooms? Yes, there is a time and a place for everything, including sitting down and being quiet, but if part of your "original equipment" involves psychomotor OE, then sitting still for 7 hours of classroom time is a form of legal torture.

Sensual Overexcitability

Sensual overexcitability should not be confused with raging hormones, that adolescent affliction attributed to any teenager with an emerging libido. Nor is sensual OE a quality observed only in older children, for it can be noted in even the youngest of kids. For example, do you have a child who cuts the labels off T-shirts because the tags are just too itchy? Do you have a child who smells everything before she eats, wears, or plays with it, announcing, "I like it" (or not), from this mere olfactory experience? Do you have a child who asks the teacher to turn off the fluorescent lights because the incessant buzzing is a constant distraction that doesn't seem to bother anyone else? Do you have a child (or spouse) who avoids the perfume area in any department store for fear of getting an unwanted, headache-inducing spritz from one of those annoying employees paid to spray unsuspecting victims? These sensually aware individuals have fine-tuned sensory systems that are bombarded by stimuli constantly, each one attractive or repellent in its own unique way.

Consider this piece, written by 17-year-old Sarah, who was providing a synopsis of her to-date school and life experiences:

> My life during school, and my life to this day, has been a draining and exhilarating blur of music rehearsals, challenging classes, unwavering high grades, volunteering, working part-time, late days, long nights and little sleep. My life is a balancing act and it is a dance: vigorous, complex, continuous, orchestrated, random and always in motion. And no matter how much I may try to 'take it easy', my soul seems to know no other way of life than this. (Schultz and Delisle, 2007, p. 89)

Beautiful words and images, to be sure, from a young lady in constant sensual and intellectual motion. But, what it took for Sarah to create this passage involved more than just interesting, sophisticated wordplay. It also took an enhanced ability to sense the world from multiple perspectives—to see her world as a mad rush of oncoming, often competing, demands and (in Sarah's words) as an "exhilarating blur."

Children who are sensually overexcitable might be criticized as being too dramatic, too sensitive, too everything! To help them appreciate the beauty of this gift of insight, let them explore avenues that relish this savvy; let them paint, act, write, sing, and create images of the world that they sense in a higher key than others. To quote Kurt Vonnegut (2005), "Sing in the shower. Dance to the radio. Tell stories. Write a poem to a friend, even a lousy poem. Do it as well as you possibly can. You will get an enormous reward. You will have created something" (p. 24).

In addition to encouraging these visceral expressions of self, give your sensually OE children appropriate outlets for dealing with situations that are overly loud or boisterous. One family I know convinced their daughter's kindergarten teacher that she be allowed to leave the gym during assemblies and simply sit in the adjacent hallway. There, she reads quietly, often with her hands on her ears, until the nearby ruckus has subsided. Now tell me, wouldn't *you* do the same if you could at that rock concert or monster truck rally someone dragged you to against your better judgment? Your sensually OE child will appreciate that you value his or her right to see, hear, touch or taste in unique ways.

Intellectual Overexcitability

Having an intellectual overexcitability would seem to be synonymous with giftedness, and that is, in fact, very close to true. As I described in an earlier publication,

> The intellectually OE person is a minefield of exploding thoughts. It is someone who is curious, mentally alert even when relaxing, driven to absorb and understand any new idea, and someone who likes any type of intellectual challenge, be they word games, three-dimensional puzzles, or the College Championship segments on *Jeopardy!*. The intellectually OE child will be in bed at the appropriate bedtime but will more likely than not be reading under the covers with a flashlight. (Delisle, 2005, pp. 222–223)

Always asking "Why?" even from the youngest of ages, and not being satisfied with pat answers that are incomplete or simply not true, intellectually OE people are on cognitive overdrive constantly. They are challenging, too. Not afraid to take on untruths that are disguised as "authority," they will correct their teachers, their parents, and their friends. They point out inconsistencies in thinking and will be among the first to recognize when the Emperor is not wearing any clothes. Stupidity makes them angry. Illogic makes them cringe. Political gamesmanship makes them question the merits of democracy.

The best thing that parents can do when confronted by intellectually OE children is to listen. They will share theories and ideas. They will read to you page after page of their latest favorite book so you can gain a flavor for its importance. They will complain about adults who offer wrong information, but refuse to admit it even when presented with a factual rebuttal. And, if they are in a school that neither challenges them nor appreciates their willingness to argue, they will beg you to send them elsewhere or to begin homeschooling. Here's what one 7-year-old girl wrote to me about her dissatisfaction with school:

> Every school day is very easy for me. Even though my class is all gifted kids, I am still very bored in class, causing disruptive and obnoxious behavior. Also, I am the only 2nd grader in the Semantics Club. My favorite part of school is reading because every book I open is an adventure into the land of questions, answers, connections and thoughts.

Of course you should encourage your gifted child's abundant love of learning, but let your son or daughter know something else, too: that there is a time and a place for everything. So, it is better to go to a teacher after class and correct her syntax privately, rather than do it in front of 25 other seventh graders. And, when the school principal imposes a punishment on everyone for the faults of a few, shouting out "That's neither right nor fair" in the cafeteria probably won't win you any gold stars for comportment. Also, let your gifted kids know that the bus ride home is probably not the best time to inform your classmates about the distinction between a Russian and a Prussian. And finally, forget about correcting Dad's grammar at the dinner table when he is retelling (again) his favorite story about growing up in Appalachia. Going back to Hollingworth's (1942) notion of suffering fools gladly, these situations would be handy-dandy times to recall her warning about getting martyred by the mob.

Can someone be gifted and *not* overexcitable intellectually? That depends on your definition of giftedness, of course. I've long made a distinction between being a naturally and perpetually curious gifted kid and a high-performing achiever who informs you that you simply need to "tell me how to earn the A, and I'm outta here." From my admittedly biased perspective, this latter example does not connote giftedness but simply a striving for a grade that moves a person along the educational treadmill. Missing the richness that accompanies an intellectually OE person, a high achiever like this is no more gifted to me than any scribbled sketch is a Picasso.

Imaginational Overexcitability

If you live with a child who possesses imaginational OE, your life is filled with frolic. Your imaginative child lives in the kingdom of creativity, manufacturing parallel universes and inventing friends who live in them. When asked at school to name four basic food groups, your child might respond, "Burger King, Pizza Hut, McDonald's, and Wendy's," just because it is a more interesting answer than the typical one teachers seek. In your child's mind, the only thing absurd is the ordinary, the only second language worth learning is one you've invented, and the most important question that is ever asked is not "Why?" but "Why not?" His or her idols are comedians, poets, architects, and anyone else who takes the typical and makes it less so.

There is also a painful part of being an imaginationally OE child—lots of people don't "get you." These children's humor is often tinged with irony or double entendres, and these children may guffaw at situations that those with less active imaginations fail to see as funny. A case in point: Six-year-old Cassie was watching a movie on schoolyard safety being shown by her physical education teacher. As the teacher went to turn off the VCR, he tripped over the power cord, falling face first into a first grader's desk. While the rest of the children showed concern about the teacher's safety, Cassie was trying unsuccessfully to stifle a very big laugh. While being admonished by the classroom teacher for laughing at someone's misfortune, Cassie tried to explain (also unsuccessfully) that she found it hilarious that the PE teacher got hurt while showing a movie about safety! Her humor fell far short of impressing the teacher, and a punishment was imposed. I guess when you are 6, you are not supposed to see the humor in situations that would make most adults laugh out loud.

On a less humorous note, let's consider Brett, a high school senior whose English class assignment was to compose an essay describing his experiences and goals as a writer. In a 500-word expression of his views, Brett said things like this:

> Let's get one thing out of the way—I'm lazy. I've never been the overachiever or the 'A' student. I honestly don't care about some letter on a paper judging work that I didn't care about in the first place. I used to have a passion and fire for the written word; I wasn't complete without a pen in my hand. Then the public education system killed my passion in cold blood. Prompts, essays and written responses were the beasts that killed my love of the art. You'll see me in the back of the room, drawing. It is the only thing I care about anymore, for the assassins that once destroyed my passion for writing will not do the same with my art. For me, school is now only a twisted prison, filled with others like me whose dreams were pounded out of them by the harsh mallet of conformity.

Brett's teacher didn't comment on the passion this young man obviously possessed in abundance. Instead, she told him that his essay needed an introduction and conclusion, giving him an unexplained 45 points out of 50. Imaginational OE was dismissed, if it was even recognized at all, by an educator whose compliance to conformity proved Brett's point about his dissatisfaction with his English education.

More than anything else, what imaginational OE kids like Cassie and Brett need are educators and others who will encourage their creative sparks and not let them die among cries to "get real," "return to Earth," or "think logically, for a change." Put down by a society that only respects creativity when it does not press too strongly on accepted norms, the imaginationally OE child is in danger of repressing this fragile gift to satisfy the swarms of others who wear creative blinders. If you have a Cassie or Brett in your life, remind him or her that it is fresh ideas and innovative spirits that will take our world into places not yet reached by conventional thinking. Given a choice of having his or her imagination channeled or cherished, always go with the latter.

Emotional Overexcitability

The final OE is called *emotional overexcitability*. The emotionally OE child is the one who befriends stray cats or kids who look funny "because someone needs to like them." They want to know why world peace is considered a pipe dream instead of a reachable goal, and they don't understand why politics has to impede common sense. They possess a rare and uncanny ability to transform their own lives and act in accordance with principles that are bigger than they are.

I witnessed an emotionally OE young child in action when I was doing work at an international school in China. It was only a month before the end of the school year, and the school's kindergarten teacher had just received a letter telling her that her work visa would not be extended and that she would need to leave China when the current school year ended. Upset at receiving this news, this teacher was in tears, being consoled by a colleague. Not far away, 5-year-old Maya noticed something was wrong, and wrote this poem for her teacher:

There is harmony in the tears of love.
There is melody in the tears of laughter.
There is a breeze in the tears of sadness.
There is a snow in the tears of missing people.

I have no idea where this sensitivity comes from when you are 5 years old—or 40 years old, for that matter—but I *do* know that this emotional gift is as spectacular as it is rare. Yet once it is noticed, it must not be ignored.

A more clinical interpretation of what an emotionally OE child like Maya is like would read like this:

She has . . .

- intense positive and negative feelings;
- an awareness of the emotions of others;
- strong physical reactions to situations that are wrong and need to be corrected;
- feelings of guilt and shame about being unable to control events that impact others negatively;
- a capacity for developing strong attachments and deep relationships; and
- a concern with life, death, God, and spirituality.

The list could go on, but it probably doesn't need to, for if you are the parent of one of these emotionally enriched children, you have already seen him or her in these statements.

It is my contention, backed more by frequent observation of gifted children than by research proof, that emotional OE is the cornerstone of all of the other excitabilities and is frequently the most profound of all of them. Emotional OE may be interwoven with the other OEs, so that a child who cries in pleasure at the sound of a symphony orchestra is exhibiting rich human emotion brought on by a sensual experience. Seldom selfish and often altruistic, children with emotional OE can become either zealots for righteous causes or embittered to inaction by the barriers put up by others who neither see nor care about inequity or discrimination. More than anything else, gifted children with emotional OE are people you are proud to know, as they possess a rare and uncanny ability to transcend their own lives and act in accordance with principles that are bigger than they. As spouses, parents, community leaders, and quiet advocates for those without a voice, their actions improve a world very much in need of their insights and intensities.

However, too often, when confronted with an emotionally OE child or adolescent, especially one in "meltdown mode" over an especially wrenching experience, kindhearted adults do the wrong thing: They try to take away or diminish the importance of the individual's intensity by saying things like "Don't worry about it," or "Things will be better tomorrow," or chastising the person for "always taking things so seriously." Not surprisingly, none of these reactions is helpful.

Instead, I offer advice from author Anne Lamott (2013), who suggested an alternative:

> As far as I can recall, none of the adults in my life ever once remembered to say, "Some people have a thick skin and you don't. Your heart is really open and that is going to cause pain, but that is an appropriate response to this world. The cost is high but the blessing of being compassionate is beyond your wildest dreams. However, you're not going to feel that a lot in 7th grade. Just hang on." (para. 3)

Repeat after me: "Just. Hang. On." These three little words give your gifted child permission to mourn, to feel sorrow, or to simply wallow in an intense bout of emotion. Recognizing this intensity without trying to downplay its importance is one of the greatest gifts you will ever give to a child like this. And once this child or adolescent knows that you respect his or her heightened emotionality, you will be richly rewarded. Indeed, you will know the true meaning of joy.

The Journey Begins . . .

Each of the OEs described here helps us to understand more fully the inner world of the gifted child. Some would call these abilities *emotional intelligence*, a term coined by Daniel Goleman (1995) in his best-selling book of the same name, but it was Michael Piechowski who took this idea a step further by postulating that the OEs are not a *supplement* to the gifted child's personality, but the *true essence* of it. Just as one hand enfolds the other to create a cocoon of warmth, the OEs, when combined with heightened intelligence, create an individual who is capable of both great insights and profound compassion; it becomes hard to distinguish whether the genesis of one's enriched abilities is in the head or the heart. Listen to one father describe his son's reaction to an everyday event:

When David was 8, he was looking at a picture of his Cub Scout den from a skit they did. David noticed that there was not a space represented in the name "Tiger Cubs." Each boy had one of these letters, and then stepped forward to say something like "T is for Teamwork," etc. The conversation went something like this:

"Dad, we should have had a space, because "Tiger Cubs" is two words."
"You're right, David, but who would want to be a space?"
Five minutes later, David returned and said, "Dad, they could say:
'I am a space
I separate Death and Life
Joy and Sadness
Good and Bad
Warmth and Coldness.'"

David did this within one week of his eighth birthday. (personal communication, March 18, 2003)

Was David *taught* how to see this clearly? Did he learn from watching and listening to older children and adults as they explored complex, abstract ideas? If these questions have definitive answers, I have yet to find them. However, such discovery is not the point. Instead, we must realize and accept a simple truth: The giftedness expressed by our children is a quality no more universal than being tall or blue-eyed, and it is no more present in everyone than is having an ear for music, an eye for art, or a heart for empathy. Most importantly, you cannot *train* someone to be gifted; you can only cherish and protect the insights and visions they possess naturally. In essence, gifted children *simply are*.

Too frequently in my educational career and in my role as a dad of a gifted son, I have heard naysayers bemoan the entire concept of giftedness, spouting a bromide like "everyone is gifted in some way, you know." Well, actually . . . that's not true. To be sure, every living being is a unique entity, entitled to individual appreciation and respect for whatever level of talents and passion they possess. But that does not equate to everyone being gifted, just as being able to point out the constellation Orion in the night sky doesn't make one an astronomer, nor does enjoying a crisp glass of French Bordeaux qualify someone as a sommelier. Giftedness, as a concept and a life condition, is not distributed equally to all, as much as our egalitarian selves would like to make it so. Believing this truth doesn't make you elitist, just accurately informed.

In closing this chapter, I have to wonder if you envisioned the discussion of giftedness going in the direction that it did. Most books about giftedness review in overblown detail the intricacies of IQ and achievement tests and the benefits and flaws of each in the identification of high intelligence. Instead, I took you on a different kind of ride and led you, I hope, to a different kind of place. The destination I sought for you was self-discovery that involved a vision of giftedness more complex yet, ironically, less well-defined than most. Pinpointing the definition of giftedness is hard, but knowing when you see it is easy. As Michael Piechowski (1991) wrote,

> When gifted people, and those who live and work with them, are introduced to these OE concepts, there is often an instant recognition and a sense of relief. It helps to find out that there is a theoretical model that makes sense out of a manner of feeling and acting that is so often at odds with normal behavior and expectations of happy—or grim, as the case may be—adjustment. It helps for once to feel legitimate in one's "abnormal" reactions and what one cannot help experiencing and wanting to express. (p. 287)

The formation and fruition of the OEs are lifelong in nature. For better or for worse, they are never outgrown. More on that in a later chapter on adult giftedness (see Chapter 7).

Gifted Children Speak Out

"I've found that one part of my personal myth is the belief in myself, my abilities, and my thought processes. I am a spiritual being, capable of great wisdom, deep thought, and personal happiness. I look into myself for answers, and often find pieces of myself that I never realized existed. I put them into the puzzle of my life, and hope that one day the masterpiece will be complete."

—Boy, 17, Maine

"I need to have time to just be alone in order to think. This seems weird to my parents. They expect me to want to be doing things with friends, but having down time to me is the greatest pleasure in my day. I can sort out some of the many ideas floating around in my head. Without time to do this, I get very moody and mean."

—Girl, 16, Florida

"Being alone gives me time to decompress. I need time to sit and just stare out the window, or walk in the woods to clear my head from the day's activities. Don't get me wrong, I am a sociable kid, but I need time away from all the pettiness of being a teen to get a handle on myself."

—Boy, 15, Indiana

Chapter 4

Your Gifted Child's Education

Getting It Right

My K–8 education was in a small Catholic school with huge class sizes. A neighboring parochial school had burned to the ground when I was in fourth grade, so all of its students descended upon our building, swelling our numbers even more. Looking back, I cannot fathom how one young nun was able to teach and control the more than 50 of us who sat in her combined fourth- and fifth-grade room for the better part of two years.

But, I do remember this: Sister Patricia broke the rigid stereotype of grade-level placement by allowing those students who could handle the lessons to migrate from one side of our classroom to the other. So, in handwriting, I was still in fourth grade —and, given my lousy script, even today should still be!—but in spelling and reading and math, I was in fifth. It finally got to the point where my seat was changed permanently, and I was placed in the classroom's middle row, the one that mingled together kids from both grades. "Just listen when I teach the fifth graders," Sister Patricia whispered to me, "I think you'll do just fine."

Thus was my first exposure to grade and content acceleration, and to a teacher who understood the benefits of both.

Of all of the complaints you are bound to hear from your gifted children about school, boredom is likely going to top the list. This may not happen if they are placed in a classroom filled with other gifted students—although boredom can still occur there—but unless they have a teacher like Sister Patricia, who realized that my readiness to learn was at a different level than most of my fourth-grade classmates, boredom is a frequent byproduct of the age-regimented system that still has its stranglehold on gifted kids' learning in the majority of schools.

Occasionally, your gifted children's boredom will be feigned, as when they are just not appreciating content that is, indeed, at their level but is not on their radar screens in terms of interest. Too, there will be times when a gifted child says, "I'm bored," as justification for not doing homework that, frankly, they *do not* know how to do. (When you're a smart kid, it's tough to admit any academic gaps to others.) And, of course, there are those gifted kids who say they are bored because it is just the cool thing to say in front of their classmates. Hey, who wants to hang out with a gifted geek who begs for additional learning matter the way Oliver pleaded for more food ("Please, sir, I want some more worksheets.")?

Often, though, the gifted child's boredom is justified. Gifted kids wait around for others to finish work that they completed in half the allotted time; or they are taking their umpteenth quiz on state capitals in fourth grade, even though they could recite and locate each one by the end of kindergarten; or they are being asked to regurgitate who was who in the Civil War, rather than discussing if that war eradicated racism or simply made it take on more subtle forms after Reconstruction.

One thing is certain: In an era where federal legislation and state-level mandates prescribe that all children learn to read, compute, and compose at preset, minimal levels, the needs of gifted children are being bypassed. As we try to determine ways to reach those students with legitimate academic struggles, we are (choose your term):

neglecting . . .
ignoring . . .
caring less about . . .
slapping in the face . . .

those children for whom learning comes rapidly and readily. In too many instances, the educational needs of gifted children are forgotten or sidestepped, as our collective emphasis in schools is not to measure how tall the tree, but how short the stump. If you've ever heard a school teacher, administrator, or board member say something like, "We don't need to worry about gifted kids—they're smart enough to make it on their own," then your gifted children are at risk for not getting the appropriate instruction to help them reach the academic heights they are capable of achieving.

In an era where federal legislation and state-level mandates prescribe that all children learn to read, compute, and compose at preset, minimal levels, the needs of gifted children are being bypassed.

This chapter could be one slam after another at politicians, other noneducators, and educational "experts" who think they know what is best for children even if they've been out of the classroom for years, but that's not the battle I choose to fight. After all, I've been an educator for more than 40 years, and the majority of teachers and school administrators with whom I've had the honor to work *really do* try their best to make education relevant for their students. So, in this chapter I intend to give several reasons why gifted education is in the current quagmire that it is—and has been for decades—and then provide concrete ways to advocate for your gifted children's needs in whatever school situation they find themselves, whether in an elite and expensive private school, the neighborhood high school, or Sister Patricia's classroom of 50 children.

The "Error" of Inclusion

Dalton Conley (2000), in his stunning book *Honky*, described what it was like to grow up as the only White boy in the projects on the Lower East Side of Manhattan in the late 1970s. By lying about his address to a New York City bureaucracy too large to know any better, Conley's parents managed to get him transferred to a Greenwich Village elementary school inhabited by professors' kids from New York University. His education there was different from his schooling in the slums, but was it better? Conley wrote,

> I spent so much time on my geography and math fixations that I did almost no schoolwork. The only problems that interested me were ones that weren't already solved. I had not yet learned that eight times nine was seventy-two, but I didn't care, because everybody already knew that. The time I was supposed to be memorizing multiplication tables I spent trying to break the four-color map rule. I had decided there was no point in doing anything that was not original, that wasn't big, really big. My grades were mediocre, and my teacher consistently claimed on my report card that I was not "performing up to my potential." (pp. 72–73)

So, who is the underachiever: Dalton, or the curriculum he was expected to "learn"?

I began my teaching career just a few years shy of Dalton Conley's experiences in urban schools. Back then, educators were not afraid to place children in special programs depending on their readiness to learn. Some called it "tracking," and others called it "ability grouping," but the most sensible educators called it this: "common sense." Hey, if you were ready to learn calculus as a seventh grader, or if your limited reading abilities held you back from appreciating vibrant literature, then you were placed with others who had academic levels similar to your own. It made sense then . . . it makes sense now. The end result was children being served in schools with others of "like minds," whether those students were academic superstars or strivers who had not reached grade-level prowess in particular subjects. It wasn't a perfect system, but at least teachers were serving students in milieus where the intellectual range was rather narrow: below average, average, and above average in separate classes.

Of course, this commonsense approach could not last forever. Cries of elitism and discrimination were charged by critics—several of these criticisms valid, most of them not. To be sure, in some cases, middle-class White kids inhabited the above-average class, while the class for children with learning difficulties was populated disproportionately by poor kids or kids of other ethnicities. But instead of examining how these racial and economic imbalances could be corrected by looking at children's strengths or deficiencies in nontraditional ways, the entire model of separating children by their readiness to learn was "dissed": *dismissed, discounted, distrusted.* The reaction of the gifted children affected? *Disgust.*

In lieu of these situations where a child's readiness to learn was considered the deciding factor in classroom placement, *all* kids were now thrown together into a big, messy pool called *inclusion.* More of an experiment in social change than in educational improvement, inclusion placed fourth graders who could read at the 10th-grade level with youngsters who were still learning to write complete sentences. In the middle, of course, were fourth graders functioning at levels expected for their age, and in front of them all was a teacher, a trained professional educator. Trouble is, in a situation like this, what you need is a trained professional educator who is also a trained professional juggler. Trying to manage a classroom where every type of learning style, level, or readiness exists requires much more than pedagogical wherewithal—it also requires a daily balancing act that is unattainable by even many of our most committed teachers. Given this situation and seeing a range so wide and needs so diverse in their classrooms, many teachers did what they thought was best—they taught to the middle. Sure, some kids were bored and others were confused, but what alternative was there for a teacher whose bag of educational tricks was emptying fast?

Enter the grand solution, the panacea to end all panaceas, *differentiation*! The idea was that once teachers considered each child's singular needs in their heterogeneous classroom and adjusted their curriculum to address this multiplicity of strengths and weaknesses, all problems would be solved. Differentiation promoters envisioned a Promised Land where every teacher would be so attuned to individual students' abilities and interests that, magically, student distinctions in their readiness to learn would dissolve, as *everyone* would revel in being served academically at the exact level of their current academic competence. The trouble is, like all panaceas, this one conked out. As I noted in an earlier publication, "differentiation is a failure, a farce, and the ultimate educational joke played on countless educators and students" (Delisle, 2015, p. 36).

Oops! I did it again . . . I upset an educational applecart that was supposed to be the cure-all for serving gifted children appropriately in today's schools—except differentiation was not the cure-all that its promoters declared. Instead, teachers were led down a primrose path and were told that differentiation was the way to address the needs of *all* students, regardless of current level of academic functioning. So, if gifted students needed a challenge, teachers were told to provide enrichment materials that differed from the regular curriculum. And, if some of the struggling students found grade-level work too rigorous, teachers could locate some high-interest, low-vocabulary books that taught the same content and then develop tests and quizzes that measured what these kids picked up through silent reading. Better still, teachers could have the less capable students work with the "smart kids" in cooperative learning groups. Not only would everyone learn the content, but everyone would also learn to value others' contributions to a group process, contributing to the important social skill of accepting individual differences. Despite the hype that differentiation was the be-all and end-all way to serve gifted students—indeed, *all* students—teachers found that this high-minded promise turned out to be more hollow than solid.

The frustration felt by teachers trying to perform the differentiation miracle was (and remains) palpable. I discovered this firsthand after my article "Differentiation Doesn't Work" (Delisle, 2015) appeared in *Education Week*, arguably the most prominent publication promoting cutting-edge trends in education. *Education Week*'s editor received more comments about this article than any other one in its 32-year publication history. I, too, received my fair share of comments—hundreds, in fact—and the majority of them called me names that my mother always told me were not good words to use in public: *racist, ignorant, elitist,* etc. One reader even called me a *eugenicist,* someone who wishes to create a master race by eliminating those of lesser intelligence. Geez . . . and all I *thought* I was promoting was an educational system that addresses the needs of gifted kids instead of ignoring these needs.

The error of inclusion and its "solution" of differentiation have done enormous harm . . . If schools were like hospitals, malpractice suits would be rampant.

But I did have my proponents, mostly veteran teachers who saw the differentiation trend as yet one more way to cheapen the needs of gifted kids in today's schools. As one 29-year veteran teacher wrote to me,

> You have put into print and validated the thoughts many of us have had as classroom teachers. A link to your article is quickly making the rounds on social media, mostly among teachers like me that feel nobody has listened to what we have to say . . . these days, teaching experience is discarded and discredited and replaced with theories from those who 'know better.' I feel we are lacking balance and common sense in education anymore. (personal communication, January 8, 2015)

Aren't the qualities of "balance and common sense" ones we should aspire to, in education and elsewhere, instead of eschewing them in favor of a panacea in name only?

As it is practiced today, differentiation is the equivalent of an educational train wreck for gifted students. Think of the mayhem of an emergency room on a busy summer night, where triage is overwhelmed by cases of cuts and bruises, heart attacks, sun stroke, and broken limbs—there is no one doctor who can handle well all of the conflicting, compounding needs being presented. Would you want an oncologist checking you out for glaucoma? Would an OB/GYN be the right choice for a patient with an enlarged prostate? Is a pediatrician the most effective professional to treat your mother's dementia? No, no, no. And if we don't expect such pervasive medical expertise from physicians, why should we think that a single teacher can accommodate the needs of 30+ children who present every possible learning strength and disability in a single classroom? If specialization is the norm in hospitals, shouldn't the same be true in our schools?

The error of inclusion and its "solution" of differentiation have done enormous harm to the appropriate education of gifted children—*your* gifted children. If schools were like hospitals, malpractice suits would be rampant.

Where to Turn?

The irony of this situation is that we know both the cause of the problem and some workable alternatives, yet not much is being done to correct what we know is wrong. However, in 2004, a big step forward was taken when a national report on this travesty was released. *A Nation Deceived: How Schools Hold Back America's Brightest Students* (Colangelo, Assouline, & Gross, 2004) sent out a loud cry about the abject neglect of gifted children's educations, especially in the area of acceleration practices, wherein capable children are allowed to move through curriculum at a pace commensurate with their abilities. Acceleration can take many forms—grade-skipping, early entrance to kindergarten or college, a fifth grader taking eighth-grade geometry— but the intent of every acceleration practice is to better align a gifted student's advanced academic abilities with content that matches his or her high level of content knowledge. In the first chapter of *A Nation Deceived*, the authors contended—and they had the data to back them up—that while Rome burns, educationally speaking, school leaders are fiddling away:

America's school system keeps bright students in line by forcing them to learn in a lock-step manner with their classmates.
Teachers and principals disregard students' desires to learn
more—much more—than they are being taught.

Instead of praise and encouragement, these students hear one
word—no. When they ask for a challenge, they are held back.
When they want to fly, they are told to stay in their seats.

Stay in your grade. Know your place.

It's a national scandal. And the price may be the slow and
steady erosion of American excellence. (p. 1)

Following its publication, *A Nation Deceived* got two things it
needed to make a big impact: strong praise from both conservative
and liberal education advocates, and a slew of mainstream media cov-
erage, including a multipage article in *TIME*. Heck, it even got its own
Wikipedia page, which is worth at least *something*.

Eleven years later, a follow-up publication appeared, *A Nation
Empowered: Evidence Trumps the Excuses Holding Back America's
Brightest Students* (Assouline, Colangelo, VanTassel-Baska, &
Lupkowski-Shoplik, 2015), which cited tomes of research showing
that much progress had been made in getting acceleration practices to
be more accepted in America's schools. Also, *A Nation Empowered* put
to rest many of the myths of acceleration, including these:

- *We don't know which candidates are good ones for acceleration and
  which ones are not.* Yes, we do, and we have measuring tools to
  prove it!
- *Placing younger gifted children with older ones for academic acceleration causes social or emotional harm.* Except in rare cases, this
  is just not so, in either the short or the long term.
- *Acceleration is a costly option to implement.* On the contrary, it
  is one of the least expensive ways for schools to serve gifted
  students, as no new programs need to be implemented.

- *The academic benefits of acceleration are few.* Not so—in fact, the benefits continue on beyond one's K–12 school years, opening up new avenues of learning in college and beyond.

The Acceleration Institute at the University of Iowa (http://www.accelerationinstitute.org), from which these two national reports emanated, is a source for more specific information on the benefits of the 20 different ways that schools may accelerate their most gifted students. These reports are good reads and important ones if acceleration concerns are on your parental radar screen.

No doubt, there will still be naysayer educators who downplay the importance of acceleration practices, and others who will cling to their unfounded myths about the psychological harm caused by advancing a child beyond grade-level standards. Because these same individuals usually claim to prize evidence over opinion, share *A Nation Empowered* with them; it is an important tool in your arsenal to get acceleration opponents to reconsider their points of view. Lastly on this topic: As a parent, grandparent, or guardian of a gifted child, remember that acceleration is not a race to see who can get to the end of a curriculum first. Rather, it is a beneficial and sensible way to accommodate a child whose mind is moving at a faster clip than most. Water seeks its own level and, when it finds it, it flows freely and smoothly. So does intellect.

The Underground Guide to Getting Your Way

As best I can recall, my wife and I were only once labeled as "pushy parents." Here's the story: Our only child, Matt, was a compliant and academically strong student. In seventh grade, Matt had a math teacher who decided that despite our son's straight-A average, he wasn't taking notes the way she had prescribed them to be written. In an attempt to appease this teacher, Matt would come home and recopy his notes into the teacher's format. Matt never used these notes, but because his math notebook consisted of 20% of his grade, he felt pressured to comply.

When we discovered this unnecessary exercise, which was taking 30 minutes or more each night and preventing Matt from focusing on worthwhile homework and enjoying some purposeful downtime after school, we asked him to approach his teacher about not having to complete this notebook assignment. He had done so already, he informed us, and even when presented with the logic of Matt's being a top student in this honors-level class, his teacher emphasized how her structure of note-taking was superior to his. "You need to take notes the way I tell you," she said. Matt's frustration continued, and ours began.

To make what could be a long story short, my wife and I approached this teacher—first separately, then together—about the reasonableness of her request. She treated us with the same condescending attitude that she had shown our son—"I *am* the teacher, you know"—and even when we brought our request to the principal, his milquetoast response was, "When it comes to academics, I support my staff." So, despite our combined five degrees in education and more than 60 years of combined experience as teachers, we were written off as malcontents, pushy parents who just couldn't see beyond our own child's whining.

As a result of hitting this illogical brick wall, we told Matt to choose whether or not to complete this silly assignment and that we would support him if he opted not to; whatever grade he earned in this class would be fine with us. How ironic: We gave our son permission to circumvent an educational system that we had supported for years.

Matt (and his parents) survived seventh-grade math and, much to our relief, our son encountered an eighth-grade math teacher whose philosophy was, "Hey, if he can show me how he got his answer different from my way, I'll learn something new!" Still, that school system lost two advocates when it turned a deaf ear to our reasoned request, as it refused to show us or our son the most essential element in successful school-home relationships—respect.

Perhaps this scenario is familiar to you, even if my specific example differs a bit from what you have experienced. Whether your example deals with math or science, first grade or seventh grade, you might be feeling now what we felt then: dismissed, as a parent, because your knowledge of your child's needs and abilities is ignored in deference to a belief that *all* children need to do things in certain ways and at prescribed times.

So, how *do* you get your voice heard in such ways that your child benefits from your intervention instead of getting punished for it? Here are some suggested strategies that we and other parents have used to good effect.

Never Request a Teacher, Always Request a Style

Elementary school principals hate when parents come to them and request a specific classroom teacher for their child. The problems in doing so are many. First, unless you know the teacher well, he or she might not be as good a fit as you might suspect. Remember our seventh-grade math czarina who demanded notebook conformity? Several parents *loved* her no-nonsense approach and wanted her to be their child's math teacher. When it comes to which teachers work best with what types of kids, remember: Just because a particular teacher has a glowing reputation, his or her style may not match your gifted child's needs and quirks.

Second, even if you find a teacher who is a great stylistic match for your gifted child, there are only so many "slots" in your preferred teacher's class, and most principals are reluctant to put all of the "smart kids" with the same teacher. Racial and gender balance, as well as students with behavioral or language issues, among other factors, are typically considered in class placement decisions.

Third, new teachers are hired all of the time, and veteran teachers shift grade levels regularly. Requesting one particular teacher months in advance may limit the range of good options that would be open to your child once a new school year begins. So, instead of asking for a particular teacher, I suggest advocating for something else: Request a particular *style* of teacher.

For example, say to the principal, "My daughter is a quick and independent learner and very organized. I've found she works best in situations where she is given clear direction, but then allowed to pursue her work at her own pace. Is there a fifth-grade teacher who works best with a child like my little girl?" Or, perhaps your case is more like this: "I know my son; he is bright, but he needs structure. He needs to know his limits and what is due when. He is working at about two grade levels above his class placement, so do you have a teacher who can provide a good balance of challenge and organization?"

Mentioning how your child learns best will have the principal thinking through his or her staff for a good fit much more than a request for a particular teacher would. Such an approach provides the wiggle room and the independence for the principal to make an administrative decision that is, truth be told, his or hers to make. Your nonrequest is a respectful way to get a teacher who will work well with both your child's skills and personality.

This advice works well in elementary school, but tends to be a bit less effective in middle school and downright dubious in high school. Why? In the majority of schools, as the grade levels get higher, teachers tend to specialize more with particular content or their classes are divided into "honors" and "general education" sections. Given this reality, the higher up you go in grade levels, the fewer teacher options you are likely to have, especially in smaller schools. Also, as children get older and (generally) appreciate more independence, having Mom or Dad go into school to rescue them from the Teacher from the Black Lagoon may be something they no longer appreciate.

Strike the Word Bored From Your Vocabulary

The surest way to raise the hairs on teachers' necks is to use the word *bored* in their presence. The biggest reason teachers (myself included) detest this word is its implication: that we are doing something intentionally to turn your child off of learning. In the rarest of cases, this may be true, but the vast majority of teachers do not wake up each morning with the goal of boring any of their students. Besides that, teachers can't fix bored any more than I could expect my auto mechanic to repair my car by simply stating, "It's broken." The terms *bored* and *broken* are too vague—more specifics are needed if the kid or the car is to run properly again.

The surest way to raise the hairs on teachers' necks is to use the word *bored* . . . Teachers can't fix bored any more than I could expect my auto mechanic to repair my car by simply stating, "It's broken."

If your child announces (often with dramatic flair worthy of an Emmy) that boredom is an issue, ask for details: Is the work too easy . . . too hard (yes, this can also cause boredom) . . . irrelevant to life outside of school . . . not an area of personal interest? Once you have ascertained some specifics, ask the next question, "If you could make this class better, what would *you* do?" If your child is unable or unwilling to pinpoint the direct causes of the boredom or its solution, present to him or her this reality: "I can only help you if you give me some examples—just saying 'I'm bored' is too vague."

Having this dialogue with your child helps in a couple of ways. First, it gives her some time to think about and articulate why school is dull and how it could be better. Also, it helps her to become, with some effort, part of the solution. Boredom is an enervating condition, sapping the vitality out of any potential learning situation. By giving your child the responsibility of dissecting the boredom into its component parts, you are heading in a positive direction, as you (or your child) can now approach the teacher with a suggestion or two for change.

Of course, this is predicated on your child's teacher(s) being willing to listen to reason. I find it rare, though, for a teacher to ignore a child's request for doing different, often more difficult, work if a plan is made for what is to be done, how it will be done, and by when. Too, the alternative assignments or work may have to relate to the curriculum being studied, but some teachers, if they know your child understands the basic material, will give him or her a freer rein to do something a bit more exotic or esoteric.

If your child needs any guidance in how to approach a teacher and request something different from what he or she is being asked to complete in class, look no further than Deb Douglas's (2018) *The Power of Self-Advocacy for Gifted Learners*. A long-time coordinator of gifted programs, Douglas found that for her middle and high school gifted students, the best people who can advocate for a vibrant education are the students themselves. In her book, she focused on these four principles:

1. Understand your rights and responsibilities.
2. Assess and reflect on your abilities, interest, strengths, weaknesses, and learning styles.
3. Match your personal attributes with possible options and opportunities.
4. Connect with adult advocates who can help support your goals.

If we are being realistic, it is obvious that not every attempt at self-advocacy will be successful, nor will every teacher be willing to listen, especially if the student-teacher relationship has been frayed in the past. Still, more times than not, if a gifted student takes the educational bull by its proverbial horns and approaches a teacher with specific ideas about making education more relevant, the results will be positive for everyone involved.

Know the Jargon

Every field has jargon, and gifted child education is no exception. To become legitimate jargon, the terms need multiple syllables and, even better, they should be difficult to pronounce. Here are just a few you might want to learn, as they are common terms in this uncommon field. Figure 1 provides definitions for several of these, plus definitions for other jargon you might hear in the field of gifted education:

- acceleration and enrichment (and the differences between the two);

- differentiation and curriculum compacting (hint: the latter does not deal with trash);
- Bloom's Taxonomy (not as confusing as it sounds) and higher-level thinking;
- least restrictive environment versus most appropriate environment (the first is a term from special education; the latter refers to where gifted children are best served);
- cluster grouping, self-contained classes, and pull-out programs (three of the many ways kids are grouped to receive gifted services);
- Parallel Curriculum Model, Enrichment Triad Model, Destination Imagination, Response to Intervention (RtI), Schoolwide Enrichment Model, and Autonomous Learner Model (organized plans to serve gifted students—some better than others—and none of which should be used exclusively); and
- multiple criteria, screening, and identification (know the difference), and quantitative and qualitative assessment (which all have to do with placement decisions for gifted children).

A Chinese proverb posits that "the beginning of knowledge is knowing the names of things." This is true in any field, and gifted child education is no exception. So, do your homework and bone up on the terms you are likely to encounter when you meet with the gifted education teacher or coordinator. Knowing the language, educationally speaking, helps to even out what is sometimes an uneven playing field of jargon.

Unite for a Common Good and a Common Goal

Having lived in the northern U.S. for most of my life, I understand a simple winter reality: A snowflake falling here or there doesn't alter my travel plans at all, but when a lot of these snowflakes get together, they can wreak havoc with my schedule.

Common Terms Used in Gifted Education and What They Mean to You

Ability grouping: Grouping students of like ability to work together on a short- or long-term basis.

Acceleration: Allowing students to move to a higher level of schoolwork than their age would ordinarily dictate. This can be in the form of early entry to school, placement in a self-contained gifted classroom, earning credit by passing an examination, skipping grades, completing two grades in a single year, or dual-enrollment in both high school and college. Students can also be accelerated in specific subject areas for single classes (e.g., taking seventh-grade math when the student is in the sixth grade).

Assessment: The process of evaluating student learning with standardized testing and a clearly defined portfolio of individual work samples. Gifted education teachers often attempt to evaluate student work or performance in order to tailor their teaching to student needs and interests.

Bloom's Taxonomy: Created by Benjamin Bloom in 1956, it's the classification of thinking into six levels of increasing complexity: knowledge, comprehension, application, analysis, synthesis, and evaluation.

Cluster grouping: Small instructional groups consisting of students of the same grade level who have been identified as gifted but have been placed in a classroom of otherwise heterogeneously grouped students.

Curriculum compacting: Compacting is an adaptation to the curriculum that shortens or eliminates work that students have already mastered quicker than their classmates. It allows students the additional time and opportunity they need for enrichment or acceleration options. This process is sometimes called *telescoping*.

Differentiation: Adapting the pace, level, or kind of instructional curriculum to meet each student's individual learning needs, styles, or interests.

Enrichment: Generic term for a range of challenging student learning opportunities outside of the regular curriculum. Enrichment can also take place outside of the school system.

Flexible grouping: Grouping students based on their interests and abilities on an assignment-by-assignment basis.

FIGURE 1. Common terms used in gifted education and what they mean to you. Adapted from Delisle & Lewis, 2003.

Heterogeneous grouping: Also referred to as *mixed-ability grouping*, this is when students with differing abilities, achievements, interests, perspectives, and backgrounds are grouped together.

Homogeneous grouping: Also referred to as *like-ability grouping*, this is when students of similar ability are grouped together, regardless of their age.

Identification: Various methods used to determine which students are best suited for gifted services and programs.

IQ (intelligence quotient): Measure of a child's cognitive ability that compares a child's mental age and actual age.

Learning style: A student's preferred mode of learning, such as auditory, tactile, visual, or kinesthetic.

Least restrictive environment (LRE): The educational setting where a child with disabilities can receive a free, appropriate public education designed to meet his or her needs. LRE also requires that these students be educated with peers without disabilities in the regular classroom environment.

Multiple intelligences: Originally identified by psychologist Howard Gardner, this theory encompasses different ways of learning and processing information. The eight intelligences (as identified by Gardner) are linguistic, musical, logical-mathematical, visual-spatial, bodily-kinesthetic, interpersonal, intrapersonal, and naturalistic. Each individual has relative strengths and weaknesses within these domains.

Multipotentiality: Concept that gifted children have the ability to succeed in several areas of work or study, making career selection difficult.

Pull-out programs: This is a part-time program where gifted children leave their regular classrooms to attend specialized classes with a resource teacher. Also referred to as *resource-room* and *send-out programs*.

Self-contained program: When students are grouped on a full-time basis with intellectual peers, often for consecutive years. Its aim is to promote high achievement and reduce the social and emotional issues that gifted children may face.

Standardized testing: Testing of students under identical conditions that allows for results to be statistically compared to a standard.

Tracking: Permanently grouping students by ability, such as in the "low," "middle," or "high" math group.

Twice-exceptional: Quality of being both gifted and having a physical, emotional, or learning disability.

Underachievement: School performance that falls short of a student's ability.

FIGURE 1. Continued.

Now, this may seem an odd analogy in advocating for your gifted child; first, I do not (generally) see parents as flakes, and second, the goal of advocating for your child's appropriate education is not (again, generally) to wreak havoc in the schools. The point of the snowflake analogy is simply this: There is strength in numbers. Parents of children with disabilities learned this long ago. Today, legislation is in place and budgets have swelled to make certain that the special needs of kids with disabilities are addressed. Much of the reason behind this surge in special education is that parents rose up and said collectively, "Our children are not served well in the public schools, their civil rights are being violated, and *you will* do something about it." Funny thing . . . parents of gifted children could say the same things, but they often don't.

Why not? There are a couple of reasons. First (and I realize this sounds very tacky), gifted kids do not get the "sympathy vote" that other children with special needs do. No one begrudges children with intellectual disabilities the right to be taught in ways that will help them learn as much as they can, but in comparison, when you have a "smart kid," you are likely to hear from others, "Oh! What a joy it must be to have a gifted child. You must be so thankful!" That sympathetic rug has just been swept from under you, and your impassioned cry in the wilderness for equal treatment for your child is met with raised eyebrows and an unstated "just be happy with what you've got." This lack of understanding about the specific needs of gifted children has probably caused more parents to keep their mouths closed than any other reason.

Too, when education dollars are limited, as they always are, some parents of gifted children actually feel guilty that they seek funds for kids whose needs, by comparison, may not seem as pressing as those of some other groups of children. The incorrect assumption is that "these kids are smart; they'll make it on their own." Some will, and others won't, but as a gifted child education advocate (and a personal hero of mine) wrote so poignantly:

> Failure to help the gifted child reach his potential is a societal tragedy, the extent of which is difficult to measure but

which is surely great. How can we measure the loss of the sonata unwritten, the curative drug undiscovered, the absence of political insight? They are the difference between what we are and what we could be as a society. (Gallagher, 1975, p. 9)

These important words, written almost two generations ago, are as relevant today as they were when they were first penned. Likewise, the needs of gifted children haven't changed; they still need passionate and informed advocates who will fight for their right to receive an education that is meaningful and respectful of their advanced levels of learning.

To make a purposeful difference that extends beyond the tenure of your gifted child's school career, you and other parents of gifted children must join together like my analogous snowflakes and present your views, in unison, to sometimes reluctant audiences—a school board strapped with competing demands for priorities, a principal who tells you with a glint in her eye and a cocky smile, "All children are gifted in our school," or a PTO president who doesn't believe that the topic of gifted children is appropriate for a meeting, as the audience appeal is too limited. There are two ways to start coalescing parents of gifted children into a cohesive whole; either talk to the gifted coordinator in your school district and ask to have a meeting scheduled where parents of identified gifted kids can have a forum for discussion of common issues, or review one of the many books or websites that exist about how parents can unite for the common good of their children and follow the advice of those who came before you (see the Resources section for more).

Now the bad news: I predict that 90% or more of the people reading this book will not take my advice about advocacy, citing everything from being too busy to being afraid of ruffling the feathers of the school bureaucracy. Too bad, because if you refuse to act, you will never know the impact you might have made had you taken the time to do what every other special interest group who left a dent in our society has done: speak up to right a wrong. James Gallagher's 1975 quote, cited previously, should be ample evidence that the job of getting gifted children the type of education they need and deserve is too important to leave to chance.

Conclusion

Taking charge of your child's education is likely to be a time-consuming process. Many gifted kids will float through school with nary a complaint—nor will they be learning much of anything. You need to ask yourself, "Is this good enough?" Many gifted teenagers will want you to back off and let them slide through school with easily obtained A's from teachers who don't know the extent of their abilities. You need to ask yourself, "Is this good enough?" More than a few gifted children will sleep through class, get demoted to non-honors classes due to low grades, and be called lazy by educators who have never taken the time to kindle the sparks you know are there. You need to ask yourself, "Is this good enough?"

Remember this: Parenting is not a passive process.

Each kid gets one childhood. There are no "do-overs" and no second chances to be 9 years old for just one more year. As you make your decision to intervene (or not) when you see your gifted child's needs are being ignored, or as you decide whether (or not) to applaud the efforts of any educator who takes an interest in fully challenging your child's mind, remember this: Parenting is not a passive process. Active involvement is the best way to ensure that the kid who smiles at you upon crossing the stage at high school graduation has a full mind and a grateful heart, thanks to both teachers and parents who took the time *and* who took up the charge of advocating for this often-neglected group of children: gifted kids.

Gifted Children Speak Out

"School itself isn't flexible enough to allow us to grow as individuals. Everything is very structured. If you ask for any differences you are seen as bucking the system looking for trouble."

—Boy, 11, Ohio

"Schools need to stop repeating the same thing year after year. I wish they would just move on. I wish that schools would just teach me at my level, not theirs. I wish I could have learned Latin starting in first grade, but I have to wait until high school."

—Girl, 11, Ohio

"At 18 months, I accompanied my mother to the dentist. He asked me if I liked TV, and I told him I watched *Sesame Street*. He asked what that show was, and I told him it was 'a production of the children's television workshop,' just like they say at the end of the show. Needless to say, he was quite taken aback!"

—Girl, 15, Iowa

Chapter 5

Appreciate That Less Than Perfect Is More Than Acceptable

I t was my first year of teaching highly gifted ninth graders at a school I've now been working in for the past 7 years. I'm only a 2-day-a-month teacher there (the *best* way to teach ninth graders, in my opinion), so I don't get to know the students as quickly or as well as I might if I taught them full-time. Still, the conversations I have and the relationships I form with students progress as they move on from ninth grade. With only 180 kids in the entire school, everyone gets to know one another eventually.

But on this particular day, near the beginning of the school year, I entered my third period classroom a few minutes early to find Hannah in tears, sitting by herself, her head covered by her hands. I approached her cautiously and silently. Within seconds, Hannah looked up, trying to cover her sadness with an artificial smile.

"Seems like your day is not going so well," I mused, avoiding the always awkward-to-answer question, "What's wrong?"

"It's really not," Hannah said, as she handed me a wrinkled and tear-stained paper. "Look at *this*," she said.

I uncrumpled the paper Hannah gave to me to discover a quiz she had taken a few days earlier in her English class. The grade on the top of the page was 92%.

Hannah looked up at me as I looked over her quiz. "Can you believe it? A 92%! I've *never* had a grade that low."

Pause.

Okay, dear reader, I want you to put yourself in my place. What would you say back to Hannah?:

A. "A 92%? That's a great grade!"
B. "What are you worried about? It's still an A."
C. "You're being too hard on yourself. Most kids I know would *love* to get a grade that high."
D. All of the above
E. None of the above

If you answered "E: None of the above," welcome to the world of treating gifted children who are highly anxious about their grades with tenderness and respect. If you answered any of the other responses . . . well, then I am glad that you are reading this chapter.

My "E" response? "You seem to be really upset about your grade, Hannah."

I'm no expert at jujitsu, and Houdini-like escapes from tight spots are not my forte, but I do know this: When a gifted, perfectionistic child thinks that a grade of 92% is "bad," we must respect her opinion without trying to wrangle out a positive reaction from what is perceived by the child as a major negative setback.

So, in response to my noncommittal comment back to Hannah, our conversation began in earnest. She explained that she had never had a grade lower than 100%—on a quiz, test, or report card—from kindergarten through eighth grade, so this ninth grade "failure" of 92% was as true a disappointment to Hannah as a grade of 55% might be to most other students. Her reality was that anything less than perfection was *not* acceptable. So that's the essence of this chapter's message: that less than perfect is *more* than acceptable. It is a message that may take some time for you or your perfectionistic gifted child to absorb fully, but if you remember that academic and life successes are marathons, not sprints, then maybe, just maybe, you can help the Hannahs in your life accept that academic "failures" (like a 92%) are not indictments on one's personal worth.

The Essence of Hannah's Concerns

Hannah's example can be narrowed down to just one word: expectations. We all have them for our kids, and they all have them for themselves. Our expectations for our children might differ dramatically from the expectations they have for themselves—indeed, this is more common than rare—but the issue of perfectionism in gifted people, both adults and kids, is one of the most enduring touchstones of the entire discourse on what it means to be gifted. Like it or not, many gifted individuals define themselves by their levels of outward success—100% is awesome, and 92% is worthless—and it is our job as parents and other caregivers to try to put perfectionism into its proper perspective. Again, it's a marathon and not a sprint . . . but every race begins at the same place.

Determining the fine line between what levels of performance are acceptable and what levels are not can be as difficult as trying to get a politician to give you a straight answer to even the simplest of questions. Whether in the realm of grades or behavior, we have certain expectations for our children, which may or may not match our children's own ideas of acceptability. But what gets you in trouble regarding expectations for your gifted children is when your level of acceptability is not spelled out in detail, but rather, is stated in amorphous terms that leave open too much room for interpretation. For example, saying something like "I don't care about your grades—I just want you to try your best" may sound (to you) clear and flexible, yet such vagueness is likely confusing for even the brightest child, causing a disconnect that is seldom obvious until it's too late. So, when the report card comes home replete with B's and C's, and you mention to your child that these grades are lower than you hoped they'd be, you can expect a response like this: "You told me to try my best, and I did. So what's the big deal?" And guess what: This is the response you deserve, because you didn't pay attention to the details of what constitutes an acceptable grade.

In response to this disappointing report card—disappointing to you, at least—you decide that it is time to have one of those "little talks" that never seem to work out quite as you intended. As you sit down to chat, the scene already looks confrontational to your child, and before the first tear is shed or angry rebuttal voiced, you realize the lines of communication are already as weak as a hand of 16 in Blackjack. The conversation goes something like this:

> **You:** "Son, I know you are capable of work that is better than this."
>
> **Your child:** "Dad, you just expect me to be perfect all of the time."
>
> **You:** "That's not true."
>
> **Your child:** "Yeah? How about that time I brought home a B on that science project . . ."
>
> **You:** "You mean the one you threw together at the last minute? I wasn't mad about the grade—I was disappointed with your effort."
>
> **Your child:** "Yeah . . . like all I ever do all day is just lie around playing video games. I'm in all of the honors classes, you know. Sometimes, I just need time to relax."
>
> **You:** "And you thought that relaxing until the night before your science project was due was a fine way to relieve the pressure?"
>
> **Your child:** (Big sigh) "OKAY, I screwed up. Your little gifted genius can't always cut it. Big surprise—I'm human!"

That "little talk" went well, didn't it?

What follows is either a stomping out of the room (by either of you), a final parental statement of frustration ("You're grounded until I see improvement"), or a boatload of tears. Worst of all, the situation was not resolved, and you and your child are still chasms apart in understanding each other's perspectives on what success looks like. So, in order to make sure that your next "little talk" goes a bit more smoothly, let's examine some of the underlying reasons that gifted children and their parents often differ on how high is high enough when it comes to achievement in school, followed by some specific "do's and don'ts" that will lead to some more positive outcomes.

Issue #1: The Aura of the Gifted Label

Parent perspective. Even if you knew your son or daughter was gifted from a very young age, when your impressions are later confirmed by test scores or other methods, you feel a sense of relief, as your suspicions are confirmed by school personnel who know a gifted kid when they test one. Once the label is applied, what often follows is a honeymoon period where it is worn proudly (but humbly, of course), and life goes on much as it did before the gifted label was attached to your child. Like every honeymoon, though, it ends eventually, and reality sets in: There are exams to take, competitions to enter, and academic challenges to master. It's only natural, as a parent, to assume your gifted child will excel at each and every endeavor attempted— hey, that's what being gifted is all about, isn't it? You look around at the other gifted kids, and they seem to have no trouble juggling multiple projects and extracurricular activities. Your kid will be the same, right?

Or not. Placing assumptions on your child due to a one-word label—gifted—lands you smack in the middle of the danger zone of unrealistic expectations. In your heart of hearts, you know that no gifted child, including yours, excels at everything. But when that C in math comes home, do you remember this truth, or do you cringe, even a little, at this "low grade"? When your gifted daughter gets lunch detention for "forgetting" to turn in her homework 3 days in a row, do you see this as simply a wake-up call for your daughter to get better organized, or are you afraid to show your face at parent conferences for fear that teachers will whisper, "Yes, those are the parents of the gifted girl who got detention"?

Placing assumptions on your child due to a one-word label—gifted—lands you smack in the middle of the danger zone of unrealistic expectations.

The label of "gifted" should change virtually nothing about the expectations you have for your child, in and out of school. Why? Because the label seldom comes as a surprise to you, serving more as a *validation* of your suspicions than as brand-new information. Too, the kid who had the label applied on September 19 is the same kid you tucked into bed on September 18. If he was goofy and disorganized and wore mismatched socks before being identified as gifted, he's likely to be the same even after the aura of giftedness has been noted. Keeping your expectations in check and being realistic about school performance and behaviors is a challenge. After all, when your kid with a 140 IQ forgets to take out the trash or feed the cat—again—it's natural to want to say, "Aren't you supposed to be gifted? How can you forget something so simple?" Stifle this oh-so-natural temptation, as even if it's said in jest, it may be interpreted by your child as one more indicator that you expect him to be flawless.

Student perspective. Your fifth grader is sitting in her mixed-ability social studies class, and last week's quizzes on Bulgaria's prosperity are being returned. Your daughter earned a B, which is fine with her, as she is far more interested in emerging Asian economies than those of former Soviet satellites. Still, the kid behind her—a competitive little thing—spies your daughter's B and whispers coquettishly, "Hmmm . . . I got an A on the quiz, and I don't even go to that stupid gifted program."

Slam . . . dunk. One more small but significant indicator to your daughter that this gifted label is sometimes not all it's cracked up to be.

It is not uncommon for gifted kids to be reminded that they are supposed to act gifted 24/7. Classmates and teachers alike look incredulous if a gifted child answers a question incorrectly. Also, responsibility and social maturity are assumed traits, so it's not unusual that when a gifted child joins in on the armpit chorus when the substitute teacher asks for quiet, the real teacher returns the next day and says to all, "I am especially surprised that John (yes, your John) took part in this immature activity. I count on you to be a role model, John."

Time and again it happens, in and out of school: Gifted kids are held up as the paragons of everything virtuous and academically excellent, and when they fail to meet these standards that even the adults around them would find difficult to reach, the signs of disappointment abound. Consider this not-uncommon reaction from Grandma: She gives your gifted child $5 for every A, but nothing for any other grade, while she rewards a nonidentified sibling with $10 for every A and $5 for every B because "He has to work for his grades, dear. You're a gifted child, so yours come naturally."

Given these superinflated expectations for perfect grades, behavior, and organization, it is no wonder that many gifted children feel, despite their efforts not to, that it is their job to be flawless. Disappointment follows when any level of success lower than perfection is reached (recall Hannah's "bad grade" of 92%), so much so that many gifted students regard a low A as the worst grade of all "because I came so close, but still 'failed.'" Ouch.

Given these superinflated expectations for perfect grades, behavior, and organization, it is no wonder that many gifted children feel, despite their efforts not to, that it is their job to be flawless.

Issue #2: Fear of the Future

I've been in enough classrooms in my life to know that many teachers—indeed, perhaps most—see the grade they are teaching as a dress rehearsal for something bigger in the real world. Whether it's 12th-grade English ("College is tough, you know") or fifth-grade fractions ("If you don't learn them now, you'll be behind next year"), teachers lead students to believe that the worst is yet to come.

Yet, as I reflect on my favorite teachers, I recall the ones who cared more about today than tomorrow. Mrs. Bradley made second grade special for me because we sang every day in class, for no reason at all.

Mr. Bennett, my first male teacher, extended our recess on warm, fall days so that he could teach both the boys and the girls how to throw a spiral and fake a pass. And, in 11th-grade American Government, Mr. Maloney played the song "Hey Jude" by The Beatles for our group of horny and vulnerable 16-year-old Catholic boys, informing us that the song's lyrics were not about drugs and sex, as we all thought, but dealt instead with something called "angst . . . a quality, gentlemen, from which you shall all someday suffer." I wrote *angst* down in my notebook so I would recognize it when it appeared in my life. Years later, when it did, I silently thanked Mr. Maloney for his long-ago guidance.

My point here is that when teachers or parents focus too much on the future at the expense of the present, education becomes a meaningless stepping-stone to a faraway greater good. I was never afraid to sing in Mrs. Bradley's class, and I don't recall her ever telling me that if I didn't learn "My Country 'Tis of Thee," I'd be banished from third grade. And, at the time, I might have liked Mr. Bennett because extra recess meant less time for social studies, but I recall him now because he realized the importance of football and crisp, autumn days to a boy whose own dad was often too tired to toss a few laterals in the backyard. Instead of worrying about future events over which they had no control, these teachers concentrated on the "me" that existed that day. In doing so, they gave me the confidence to play around with this serious business called education.

As you look at your own son or daughter, stepping off the bus or out from behind the steering wheel, remember that the only assurance we have is that our children are with us *right now*. We want their futures to be long and bright, and we do everything in our parental power to make that so, but if we focus so much on unknowable tomorrows, we may be giving away the greatest gift we have—today.

Can you do at home what teachers sometimes forget to do at school? Leave the bright and successful futures that many gifted children have in their sights alone for a while, remember to celebrate today's achievements and triumphs, and put today's disappointments in proper perspective. Remember Hannah, whose tale of her "low" grade of 92% opened this chapter? This ninth-grade A- in English class is not going to keep her out of Harvard; conversely, an A+ in ninth-grade English will not guarantee her a seat in that esteemed institution on the banks of the Charles River.

Your child watches your attitude toward everyday successes and mistakes carefully, and your nonverbal reactions to a less-than-perfect performance or behavior may say as much as any spoken words. So, tread cautiously if most of your remarks are punitive or psychologically threatening ("Do you *really* think these grades are high enough to get you into a *good* college?"), or if your slumped shoulders and wringing hands indicate the depth of your disappointment. Alternatively, pat yourself on the back if the verbal encouragement you give is both genuine and good-natured ("I realize you are disappointed at not winning the spelling bee, but I truly appreciate the effort you took to succeed."), or if your nonverbal "language" is as simple as a thumbs-up or wry smile when your child messes up on something that is likely to not even matter tomorrow. Simple, dumb things that let your gifted child know that "less than perfect is more than acceptable" are simple, dumb things that, in the long run, really matter.

Issue #3: The Fleeting Nature of Success and Failure

Natalie Rimlinger has a Ph.D. from Australian National University (ANU) that she should never have earned. A self-described "rebel without a clue," Natalie could add up the number of days she went to school in grade 9 because they were far fewer than the number of days she was absent. In 10th grade, she dropped out completely, moving away from home.

After a long time wandering around—literally and metaphorically—Natalie ended up working at a counseling service for Vietnam veterans and their families. At age 30, Natalie ended up in a conversation with one of the staff psychologists. As Natalie recalled several years later, "He said to me, 'You know what you're good at?' And I said 'Nothing, I'm hopeless.' And he said, 'You'd make an excellent psychologist because you're human and you've lived through it'" (Delisle, 2018, pp. 130–131).

That was the beginning of Natalie's emergence into finding a new self. She enrolled in a distance learning program and, in completing her first assignment on the history of emotions, received a grade of 98%. Hmmm . . . perhaps she wasn't so hopeless after all. With this success at her back, Natalie then enrolled at ANU, completing a bachelor's degree in psychology. Following this achievement, she looked for further challenge and found out about this degree called a "Ph.D.," something she didn't even know existed. But now she wanted one.

A few years later, this high school dropout walked across the stage at ANU to receive her Ph.D. from an institution that was willing to give Natalie a second chance. Natalie's father attended the ceremony, showing off, in Natalie's words, "his idiot grin," and his most memorable comment was "Not bad for a kid who didn't get her Year 12 Certificate" (Delisle, 2018, p. 131).

According to a quote often attributed to George Eliot, "It's never too late to be what you might have been." Eliot may not have had Natalie Rimlinger in mind when penning this truth, but it applies as much in the 21st century as it did in the 19th.

I bring up Natalie's story here because it ties into the topic of expectations achieved after abundant struggle. But every coin has two sides, and there are also those individuals—perhaps your gifted child— who do everything right in school and still end up disappointed that they don't achieve what they had hoped. Case in point: admission to an elite university that your teenager has been spying since she was old enough to spell the word *college*.

Let's take a look at Stanford University. For admission in Fall 2018, it received 47,450 applications—up from 35,000 just 4 years prior (Stanford University, 2018). Almost every applicant was a poster child for academic excellence and extracurricular virtuosity, yet only 2,040 of them—just under 5%—were admitted. Even 69% of the applicants who earned a perfect score on the SAT were rejected. If your adolescent had been one of those denied admission after having jumped with aplomb through every academic hoop imaginable, the psychological consequences could be devastating—for you, as well as for your gifted teenager.

So what distinguished the "admits" from the "rejects," as deemed by the 50+ admission officers working at Stanford? Here's the news: "We're looking for evidence that this young person has a passion, that he or she will bring something to our community that is unique. We want to hear a voice." (Maisel, 2013, p. 1)

In an era of grade inflation and academic success at any cost, the good folks at Stanford University are saying they want something different, something less readily measured but patently obvious to those who know how to spot it: passion. Without such passion—the type that Natalie Rimlinger had to pursue her Ph.D. after an adolescence of little academic consequence—you are left with intellectually superior students who are the collective equivalent of Stepford Wives, cookie-cutter copies who sing, academically, from the same hymnal. Sorry . . . that's not good enough for Stanford. And, dear reader, it shouldn't be good enough for you.

So, what to do, as a parent, to encourage and emulate this passion? You may already know the answer, but, should it have slipped your mind, let me introduce you to someone whose entire life was devoted to the pursuit of passion: E. Paul Torrance, an investigator of creative children and adults for more than 60 years. Torrance and his colleagues created guideposts for living a passionate life, shared in Figure 2.

Post these guidelines, what I term the "Precepts of Passion," someplace obvious, and highlight in bright yellow or pink those items that matter most to you. Write and draw all over the page, and encourage your children to do the same. Discuss the meaning of these pearls of wisdom with your kids and ask them, "What the heck do these have to do with being a 9- or 12- or 45-year-old smart person?" In other words, when school is over and grades are as irrelevant as hurricane insurance in North Dakota, ask your gifted kid to consider what remains in one's life as interesting and worthwhile. You'll find, I believe, that Torrance and his colleagues hit the mark with uncanny accuracy. Following these suggestions still might not gain you admission to Stanford, but without them, you likely have no chance at all.

How to Grow Up Creatively Gifted

1. Don't be afraid to "fall in love" with something and pursue it with intensity. (You will do best what you like to do most.)
2. Know, understand, take pride in, practice, develop, use, exploit, and enjoy your greatest strengths.
3. Learn to free yourself from the expectations of others and to walk away from the games they try to impose on you.
4. Free yourself to "play your own game" in such a way as to make good use of your gifts.
5. Find a great teacher or mentor who will help you.
6. Don't waste a lot of expensive, unproductive energy trying to be well rounded. (Don't try to do everything; do what you can do well and what you love.)
7. Learn the skills of interdependence. (Learn to depend upon one another, giving freely of your greatest strengths and most intense loves.)

FIGURE 2. How to grow up creatively gifted. Adapted from Torrance, Murdock, & Fletcher, 1996.

Issue #4: The Costs of Competition

What do academics, the school orchestra, soccer, and the science fair have in common? Each is competitive. In academics, kids strive to make the highest tier of the Honor Roll. In orchestra, vying to become First Chair can be a cutthroat competition. In soccer, who doesn't try to make it onto the traveling team? And in the science fair, students try to outdo one another's trifold masterpieces to earn the blue ribbon for excellence. Competitions like these are embedded in our culture in so many ways that it is difficult to come up with a group activity where the end result does not produce winners and losers.

To some people, all of this competition is just fine. After all, in the adult world, we compete for jobs, prestige, and recognition. Whether it's the spiffiest house, the largest SUV, or the greenest lawn in town, it is the rare capitalist who doesn't want just a little more, a little better, than the Joneses next door. If we weren't a competitive society, we'd turn off the Super Bowl and watch the Discovery Channel instead.

But, what happens when the competition becomes the goal in itself, rather than the happy result of striving to do well? One kind of competition goes so far that it actually has a term applied to it: *counterfactual thinking*. In counterfactual thinking, a person believes that winning is the only reward, and if winning is not guaranteed, then that individual will put in minimal effort so as not to be embarrassed by not coming out on top. Researchers at Cornell University (Medvec, Madey, & Gilovich, 1995) studied this phenomenon with Olympic athletes. Here's what they did: They videotaped and then analyzed the facial expressions of silver and bronze medal winners in both 1995 and 2004. Almost without fail, the bronze medal winners showed genuine joy in their facial expressions, while the silver medal winners were much less facially effusive: They smiled, politely, but with little semblance of joy. Imagine . . . coming in second place *in the world* in your particular Olympic event and still feeling that your silver medal is not good enough. Another example of the mania attributed to winning at all costs is the popular T-shirt slogan, "Second place is the first loser." Gifted kids are not immune to the media messages received about the negative connotation of coming in second place, and, without our guidance, they may not choose to compete at all—in academics, orchestra, soccer, or science fairs—for fear of looking silly or "not good enough" unless they rise to the top of the heap. It seems to me that, collectively and culturally, we have lost sight of the original intent of 99% of our competitions—to have fun, to improve skills or knowledge, and to share camaraderie with others who enjoy what we enjoy. But in this insidious climate of "win or else," many gifted children who fear the embarrassment of not being No. 1 opt out of the game. They sit on life's sidelines more out of fear than disinterest, which is actually a greater loss for us all.

Although it would be unrealistic to insulate our kids from everything competitive, we can attempt to balance these win/lose situations by doing simple things with our children that emphasize the importance of simply being who they are. For example, have you ever watched your daughter's eyes when you tell her a story in which she is the hero? Do you recall the glow on your son's face when you combed through the piggy bank with him, looking for that 1948 D penny that would complete his entire set for that decade? Have you watched your teenager being taken aback when you ask, "So what's your opinion on . . . ," and then you really listen to the answer?

Be silly together. Share meaningless secrets you promise to keep. Send your kids a newspaper clipping at college about an elementary school buddy who just got married. Put a happy face note in their lunchbox—daily! Wear Scooby Doo pajama bottoms (not in public). Admit when you are at fault. Tell them when you are feeling bad, and why. Back them up when they are committed to a cause, even if it's one you don't believe in. Tell them you are always proud to be their parent at a time when they least expect to hear it. Show up when you say you will, and stay away when you promise to do so. Have a race to see who can blow the most bubbles through a straw in a glass of chocolate milk.

Okay, so this last one *is* competitive but, on balance, the others are not. And, that is the key word—balance—for when gifted children are put into competition because they are so smart, so capable, such strong leaders, they need to have downtime where they can do absolutely nothing except mess around. Or blow bubbles.

Be silly together. Share meaningless secrets you promise to keep. . . . Tell [your children] you are always proud to be their parent at a time when they least expect to hear it.

Now that I've gotten you used to being silly and (for a while) noncompetitive, let's consider a time-tested strategy that is gaining newfound popularity in schools, camps, and yoga studios alike: mindfulness exercises.

Issue #5: Time to Chill Out

Mindfulness has likely been around since Neanderthals trod the Earth. After taking down a mastodon or hunting for berries from dawn to dusk, our distant ancestors likely sat around in a cave and simply closed their eyes, breathing in deeply the nonpolluted air they were privileged to enjoy. These Neanderthals probably didn't chant, and there likely was no shaman around to guide their efforts, but quiet, introspective regrouping was likely a good way to end a prehistoric long day.

What worked then to quiet the mind still works today. Mindfulness has become increasingly popular over the last decade, and for good reason. Just look around: With today's online access to information that used to take some time to discover, children learn about the world's joys and catastrophes in the same instant that their parents, teachers, and nation's leaders do. We, as adults, can no longer filter out the type or amount of information our children are exposed to about natural or man-made disasters. To gifted children who often worry too much about things that they cannot control, this instant newsfeed can heighten their already abundant anxieties. That's where mindfulness exercises can come in handy.

The Cambridge Dictionary defines mindfulness as the "practice of being aware of your body, mind, and feelings in the present moment; thought to create a feeling of calm." There are countless other definitions, but this one seems reasonable and workable. Its specific use with gifted children is advocated by many, including gifted education specialist Michele Kane (2011), who wrote that mindfulness exercises can help relieve three types of stress in gifted individuals:

1. *Situational stress*, including a lack of challenge and conflicts between our values and those of others.
2. *Self-imposed stress*, which may involve setting too-high expectations or buying into others' negative evaluations of you.
3. *Existential stress*, including the fear of global catastrophes like nuclear war, the anxiety caused by social isolation, or the unending search for life's meaning and purpose.

I've seen the positive impacts of mindfulness activities because I have done them for more than 6 years at a summer camp for gifted children and teens, Camp Yunasa (*Yunasa* is the Lakota Sioux word for "balance"). For 90 minutes each morning—yes, 90 minutes—my colleagues and I work with mixed-age groups of gifted children on a process called *psychosynthesis*, a procedure developed by Italian psychiatrist

Roberto Assagioli more than 60 years ago and described fully in the book by Piero Ferrucci (2009), *What We May Be*. Psychosynthesis, a form of mindfulness training, is designed to bring balance and integration—synthesis—to oneself through a series of guided visualizations. Each exercise lasts between 5–15 minutes and may involve visualizing yourself steering a boat to an unknown place, meeting a master teacher who will teach you everything you need to know about a topic of your choice in 3 minutes time, or aiming and releasing an arrow toward its intended target. Following each quiet exercise, the "travelers" discuss the journey they just took, the people they met, and the ease or difficulty of completing the exercise. Deep breathing is the introduction to each activity, closed eyes are optional, and if sleep happens to occur during one of the longer scenarios, that's okay.

Some of you may be thinking that psychosynthesis resembles a séance more than a summer camp, which is exactly what I thought prior to first using it with gifted kids. What I found, though, was that even the most highly stressed "I don't want to do this wrong" type of kid eventually succumbs to the pleasure of being alone with his or her own quiet thoughts, meandering to make-believe places filled with whatever wonders exist there. During the school year, I do psychosynthesis regularly with my own ninth graders who choose to give up a bit of their lunch break to simply relax and reflect within the confines of their own imaginations. Their smiling expressions when I ring a Tibetan chime at the end of the exercises tell me that psychosynthesis is a gift that they can carry with them way beyond lunchtime.

Take it from this skeptic: Mindfulness training is a beneficial way to quiet one's often too-active mind. As a parent, you can be your child's guide through these relaxing exercises initially, but I can guarantee that it won't be long before your child will want to be the guider, and you, the recipient of his or her comforting words.

Now for Something Completely Different . . .

Now that I've gotten you all relaxed and cozy after describing mindfulness, it's time to shake things up a bit and move in a different direction. The following are some *lame statements* that you (like I) are probably guilty of saying to your gifted child at one time or another. When you first state them, you may actually think they sound appropriate. But upon reflection, and after noting your child's reaction to these lame statements, you will likely feel otherwise. In your defense, you probably stated these things because you had the best interests of your child at heart. But you know where the road paved with good intentions leads, right? So, with full knowledge that you might feel worse after reading this next section, I present four statements you should never say to your gifted child.

Lame Statement #1: "You're a smart kid, but you are not working up to your potential."

The reason this statement tops the list of the all-time worst things we say to smart, underperforming kids is that it is so vague it gives absolutely no clue as to how a child might improve. Potential exists in the eye of the beholder, and there is no clear line of demarcation that separates meeting your potential and not meeting your potential. Certainly, grades are not good indicators, as many gifted children receive A's they didn't deserve (for they did little work to get them), and yet, others have struggled to attain a C in Latin IV. Which is worth more—the lazy A or the hard-earned C? Also, when we use the "potential" argument, we often do so with a certain smugness that turns our kids off immediately. This smugness may not be obvious to you, but it is to them. Here's why: By stating "you are not working to your potential," there is an implicit message that we, the all-knowing and wise adults, realize what our kids' true potential is, and when they reach it, we'll tell them. Our game, our rules. But, if you think about it, do we really know the extent of our children's talents? For that matter, do you even know the extent of *your own* potential? Don't these indicators change over time, as access to new information and interests causes our kids (and us) to achieve great things in some areas, but not others? Potential is a variable, not a constant, yet we treat it as if it were forever the same.

If you believe your gifted child can do better than present efforts show, you might say something like this instead: "Simon, let's take a look at the work you'll be doing over the next 9 weeks in school. Which subject do you feel you can improve in, and how can I help you reach your goal?" Yes, it's still a sneaky way of kicking your kid's academic butt up a notch, but at least it focuses on specifics, not amorphous generalizations. Specific goals are the only ones ever reached.

Lame Statement #2: "You did a great job, but . . ."

Everyone knows someone like my Aunt Stella. She is like a motorist who causes an accident, but drives away oblivious to the mayhem left behind. Here is just one example of her poise. When I received my Ph.D. at age 28, I was the first in my extended family to get a doctorate. Upon receipt of my degree, my parents sponsored a party, Aunt Stella being one of the guests. As she drank her white zinfandel (ugh) and gobbled down the chicken fajitas, she gave me the kind of praise Aunt Stella is known for.

"Jimmy," she said, "we are so proud of you. You have accomplished so much." She took a minute to chew . . . okay, 2 minutes. "Just one thing makes me sad," she added. "Why didn't you become a *real* doctor? You always had the brains to become a *real* doctor." She shrugged her shoulders and squeezed my cheek. "But we're still proud of you for this Ph.D. thing, although I don't understand what you'll do with it."

If I had become a "real" doctor, I am convinced I would have gone into pediatrics, because I've liked kids since I *was* a kid. Aunt Stella's likely evaluation of my pediatric preference? "You had the brains to be a surgeon."

Your child has met Aunt Stella already—many times, perhaps. The world's Aunt Stellas are not cruel; they are merely misinformed. They believe they have the best interests of gifted children at heart by always urging them to look ahead at what's next rather than examining what is good about what lays right in front of them. They second-guess every decision and every triumph, letting your children know that with a little more time, effort, or enthusiasm, they "coulda been a contenda."

One simple, single word—*but*—is one of our language's natural depressants, dampening a compliment the way a rainstorm ruins a picnic. *But* diminishes the importance and worth of even the most genuine compliment that preceded it, erasing any semblance of pride a child might have accepted as credit for a job well done. In a very real way, it becomes a kick in the "but."

The solutions are easy. First, tell your children that the reason they have two ears is so that some things that enter one of them can exit the other side without ever stopping in the middle of their minds. So, when an adult who really doesn't know your children (Aunt Stella never knew me, although she thought she did) gives them a kick in the "but," remind your kids that they have your permission to ignore that adult. This is not being impolite, but merely practical, for if *every* smart kid has to listen to *every* urge to improve from *every* person who thinks he or she has the right to offer an opinion, your gifted child will be inundated with confusion and anxiety.

On the other hand, if the "*but* culprit" is you or someone near and dear to your child's existence, the solution is also pretty simple—keep your mouth shut. Instead of saying "You did a fine job on that report, *but* if you had used five more references you might have gotten an A," simply say, "You did a fine job on that report." Period. End of sentence. The compliment stays intact. Should you feel strongly that you *still* need to prod your child to do better, that's fine. Just do so at a later time, after the glow of the compliment for a fine job has been absorbed.

Lame Statement #3: "This'll be easy for a smart kid like you."

Here's the scenario: Your child has decided to take an advanced class at school, and you are very pleased, especially because the subject is calculus—your favorite! You know you will be able to help with homework in a meaningful way.

Class begins, and shortly thereafter, so do some problems. Where previous classes have been pretty easy, this one challenges your teenager, raising self-doubts about the wisdom of taking such a tough course.

"Time for me to intervene," you think. So you do. Dredging up your knowledge of things mathematical, you begin to help with homework. When your captive audience (i.e., your teenager) hits snag after snag, you watch the frustration and offer a word of advice. Hugging a now-slumping shoulder, you say, "I know this is new to you, but you can grasp it. In fact, in time this'll be easy for a smart kid like you."

Ah . . . I can already smell an argument brewing, probably beginning with, "Just because I'm smart, it doesn't mean . . . "

Unintentionally, you just made a gifted kid feel dumb by suggesting that a concept that was personally difficult to grasp for him or her should actually be pretty easy to understand. Your teen's inner thought becomes, "Hey, if this stuff is so easy and I can't get it, I must be more stupid than I thought. Maybe I'll drop the class." It may have been inadvertent, but your words still stung, especially if your child was honestly trying to grasp an elusive concept that was crystal clear to you.

Instead of using the "smart kid" strategy, say something like this: "I can see you're having some difficulty understanding this concept. It is quite complicated. If it's okay with you, I hope that we can work on it together until you feel comfortable with it." This message validates your teen's efforts and acknowledges that calculus is difficult. Also, it indicates that even smart kids will have to struggle with new material sometimes, a situation that may be fairly rare in your child's prior educational experiences.

Lame Statement #4: "I don't care about your grades as long as you try your best."

I alluded to this comment earlier as being a confidence killer, but it is such a big issue to consider, that I want to reinforce it and elaborate on it again. Generally, this statement is said when a new academic venture is undertaken by a child who is unsure how well she will do. What happens, though, is a communication mix-up, as your child may misinterpret *your* best as *the* best. Further, if we venture into the realm of athletics, and we ask our children to "try your best" at water polo, the interpretation may be that "best" is the only acceptable standard. Doing something for the sake of just doing it doesn't seem to be an option.

Think of the unreality of always trying your best. For example, do you try your best at every element of *your* daily, adult life—in work, in completing household tasks, in exercising? Or, do you realize that it is sometimes okay to have a house that is 70% tidy or a 4-day-a-week exercise schedule rather than a 7-day-a-week routine? Once in a while, our gifted kids need to hear from us that being average is as acceptable for them as it is for us, as adults. Trust me, as a mechanic, I am *not* average; I am downright mediocre. But, as an adult, I have the prerogative of saying those two magical words—hire out!—when faced with a task I do not want to exert my energy doing. Gifted children need the same degree of freedom to opt out of not being a top performer in everything they do and to allow others who are more skilled than they are to take over the task. There is simply not enough time and energy in anyone's life to excel at everything.

Gifted children need the same degree of freedom to opt out of not being a top performer in everything they do. . . . There is simply not enough time and energy in anyone's life to excel at everything.

Conclusion

Have I given enough examples of the many ways we go awry as parents when all we are trying to do is help? Do you feel the same sense of guilt reading this chapter that I did in writing it? Indeed, I could not have written this chapter, especially the *lame statements* section, if I was not guilty of doing or saying many of the things I am now asking you to avoid. Live and learn.

As parents, there are many things we say or do that we wish we could take back later. We, like our kids, are imperfect beings, and it would be silly to believe that even our best-intended efforts are always interpreted in the positive manner with which we offer them. So, if you find yourself in these pages, don't feel guilty or dumb, just human.

And, should you think you've done irreparable harm to your gifted kid because you leaned too heavily on the achievement-at-all-costs mantra, just backpedal a little bit and be honest with your child: "Sam, I'm sorry what I said made you feel bad. That was not my intent. Let's rewind and try again."

Life is filled with mistakes and miscalculations. That means that life is also filled with second—and third, and fourth—chances. As we venture down this path toward being as close to perfect parents as we can, let's understand how ludicrous that goal really is. It's the flaws that make us human and interesting.

In an odd way, that's comforting.

Gifted Children Speak Out

"Being gifted may be a blessing and all, but gifted students and adults have their off days, too. Even if we're up and running most of the time, we all need a break once in a while."

—Girl, 13, Nebraska

"My parents do not expect as much from me because I have had older siblings who were very intelligent, so they trust the fact that I will not make stupid mistakes and throw my life away. When other adults encounter the fact that I'm gifted, they drop most of their teenage stereotypes and ask me questions about what I like."

—Boy, 14, Ohio

"I got my first zero on a homework assignment that I had actually done, due to my not understanding my teacher's instructions. My mother hung this paper on the refrigerator and we all got a good laugh out of it."

—Girl, 19, Texas

Chapter 6

Living the Nuanced Life

In Chapter 2, I wrote about the difference between peers and age-mates, contending that gifted children often find a natural affiliation with others who are older (or sometimes younger) than they. Fifteen-year-old Jackson knew well the relevance of this distinction:

> My mom swears that I am more of a child now than I was when I was a child! Now that everyone else is studying geology and reading *Mien Kampf* [*sic*], I much prefer watching Japanese anime, playing and creating video games, and talking about cars! I imagine part of the reason is that when I was younger I had no one else to interact with. The kids in second grade got sick and tired of me talking about and showing them my collection of rocks, and the kids in third grade weren't interested in why Hitler hated the Jews no matter how hard I tried to share with them. Now, on the other hand, I have interests that coincide with people my age . . . video games, anime, cars, etc. I am never without someone to communicate with so there is little time to read books like I used to. It looks like I'm not

doing anything "important" like I used to. But hey, I'm happy! (personal communication, September 12, 2004)

What may appear to some as regression, Jackson saw as growth. An odd sort of equilibrium was reached, where Jackson's intrigue with "normal" teenage interests made him part of a group from which he was once excluded—age-mates. Time, maturity, and perspective softened the hard edges of this gifted child whose intelligence once separated him from other kids his age. Appreciating this social nuance, and being bright enough to recognize it as an asset, not a flaw, is vital to living a life that is not filled with disappointment or regret. The gifted child, adolescent, and adult share this in common—the desire to be smart and social simultaneously.

There is an oft-stated stereotype that gifted children are awkward and clumsy when it comes to social situations—that they either don't pick up on subtle social cues and monopolize conversations with random odd statements, or that they would rather sit in a corner contemplating plate tectonics than engage in banter about last night's Red Sox game. For a few gifted kids, this stereotype probably fits, but for the most part, it's a myth. As that Wonder Woman of giftedness, Leta Hollingworth, wrote, "Isolation is the refuge of genius, not its goal" (1942, p. 167). So if a gifted child (or adult, for that matter) struggles with particular social situations, it is not an intentional slam on others, nor is it necessarily a lifelong affliction; rather, it is a condition that will likely improve over time, once connections are made with both age-mates and peers. Just like it did for Jackson.

The nuances that exist in the life of a gifted individual are not limited to the social realm, though. Given the gifted child's propensity to make even the simplest things complicated, or to see gray in situations where black-and-white thinking is the norm, nuance exists in almost all aspects of a gifted child's existence. These children may question the religious tenets that have guided your life and reject some of the beliefs that you hold dear. They may argue the merits and flaws of controversial issues—abortion, the death penalty, legalization of drugs—that you are ill-prepared to talk about with a 10-year-old. And they might rebel against people who warn them of the dangers of smoking or drinking when these same adults engage in the very behaviors that kids are being told to eschew. So yeah . . . nuance complicates the life of gifted children and the lives of those adults who are trying to guide them on the path to independence and intellectual honesty. It can all be quite an interesting journey, can't it?

Let's examine some of these nuances in more detail, but be warned: You may see yourself in some of these reflections, not just the child who brought you to read this book.

Nuance #1: The Myth of Underachievement

I had really hoped that my many graduate courses in gifted child education would guide me toward a better understanding of how to work with smart kids who choose not to do well in school. That didn't happen in either those college lectures or the books I read on this subject. Instead, I learned about this so-called "underachievement" directly from the students I came to know. Here's one of them, a high school senior named Mark who originally contacted me by e-mail:

Dear Dr. Delisle:

School in ugh. Today, in sociology, we got into the topic of whether nature or nurture was responsible for development. What better way to teach us this than to give us a worksheet. It gave an opinion on the nature argument and another on the nurture, and then asked us questions about our opinions. It had the same question phrased three different ways. I looked at it and got so pissed. This teaches me nothing. I learn how to copy stuff from the front of a worksheet to the back. To me, school is trying to create the passive, submissive mold of a student who will do whatever teachers want for the sake of a grade. Ahhhhhhh!

Incidentally, this note was from a top scholar in a prestigious private school who appeared to be playing the "school game" well. However, Mark's high grades and top 10% standing in his school didn't mean that he saw his education in a positive way. He worried that filling out worksheets would be inadequate for his pending move to college, and, as he said, he was "pissed" that even an elite high school could be so immune to knowing the meaning of academic excellence.

Mark and I talked and met several times, and he helped me to adopt a new perspective on underachievement, one that allowed for the fact that, sometimes, it is not the student who underachieves, but the school system itself.

In conversations with Mark and dozens of others like him, I came to realize that the term *underachievement* is often a misnomer, as it places the "blame" of low grades or dissatisfaction with school firmly at the feet of the student. Often, though, the real culprit is the educational system, which led me to coin a new phrase that better describes smart kids like Mark who do not do well in school: *selective consumers*.

If you live with one of these selective consumers, he or she may have:

- the ability to explain why schoolwork is not good or grades are low ("Look, if they'd offer something worthwhile, I'd learn it!");
- the ability to "read" a teacher in minutes, performing for those who give students strong content and high respect ("I like Ms. Cornelius—she's cool and she respects what I know.");
- an independent intellectual streak that causes him or her to pursue interests with passion, sometimes to the exclusion of other obligations ("I know I haven't done my homework, but look at this new computer program I've designed!");
- a strong sense of self and little guilt about low grades ("I could get high grades if I chose to, but what's the point?"); and
- the ability to improve academically, sometimes overnight, with the right teacher and a flexible learning environment ("See? I told you I could do it!").

If these traits describe your "underachieving" gifted child, then the common solutions to take away her passions until she performs up to potential, or to put him on a contract so he knows what he needs to accomplish to earn a reward, or to remove her from the honors-level or advanced classes until she "proves" she belongs in them will all backfire. Why? The real problem—an unfulfilling school curriculum—is not being addressed. Only when the adults in charge take this child seriously will long-term improvements occur.

Here are some ways to address the very real concerns of smart students who choose not to perform well in school:

- eliminate or reduce significantly any work already mastered;
- allow independent projects on topics of personal choice;
- place your child with teachers who understand and appreciate gifted kids' intelligence, humor, and sarcasm;
- incorporate problem-solving techniques instead of rote, drill-to-learn skills; and
- whenever possible, combine the typical school subjects of math, science, language arts, etc., so that students see the "big picture" of how these areas overlap in real-life situations.

I put together an additional series of suggestions (Delisle, 2018) for working with selective consumers that are aimed at getting A's. These A's are not necessarily grades (although that would be fine with me), but rather, something richer and deeper: Here are the A's I suggested:

Autonomy: How can we help students engage and become the "masters of their universes" with respect to what education is and what it might become?

Access: How do we work with students to identify curricular challenges that are both meaningful and interesting?

Advocacy: How can we guide students toward becoming advocates for their own education and empower them to become their own best spokespersons?

Alternatives: What new-horizon options (e.g. home school, independent study, online courses) might be appropriate with students for whom traditional school is a bad fit?

Aspirations: How can we acknowledge and respect our students' dreams and help them to achieve their personal goals?

Approachable Educators: What personal and professional dispositions can we display that invite our students to want to learn? (pp. 34–35)

I elaborated more specifically on what these six A's entail in the book (Delisle, 2018), but I'm guessing you can add your own texture and depth to this outline. Of course, when you first enter your child's school with these suggestions, you may be as welcome as a Twinkie salesman at a dentist's convention. In fact, you may be hit with comments like these:

- "If we do what you ask, we're simply buying into your daughter's inappropriate behaviors. When she starts to turn around, we'll consider what you ask." (In other words, "no way".)
- "If we eliminate work your son knows how to do, other students will see that your son is getting away with not doing something they are required to do. That wouldn't be fair." (The fairness card is often pulled.)
- "In the 'real world' of work, your child will have to do things that aren't always exciting. Might as well get used to it now." (In other words, the world is boring, so school should be, too.)

What should you do if you hit these excuse-filled roadblocks? Persevere, persevere, persevere. If a teacher or counselor who understands your point of view is willing to be an ally in your quest, receive this help with open arms. But, if you must go at it alone . . . well, then you must go at it alone. Know that your child is worth the effort you are making, and know, too, that the more often you can remind school personnel that you all share the common goal of success for your son or daughter, the more open-minded they may become. And then, if you reach nirvana, and the school gates are opened wide to accommodate your ideas for reversing this pattern of so-called underachievement, have a major heart-to-heart with your daughter about her role in making this plan a success. Without effort on her part, and a "buy-in" that she is essential to a positive solution, the likelihood of returning to the "same-old, same-old," in terms of school requirements or structure, is an inevitable, unworkable outcome.

What should you do? Persevere, persevere, persevere.

One last thing: I know that it is frustrating to parent a gifted kid who doesn't perform highly in school. However, the one thing you must not do, *under any circumstances*, is be willing to sacrifice your parent-child relationship for the sake of a grade. I've seen this happen way too often, where a division between a parent and a child occurs due to low school performance. So you need to remember this: That inquisitive, young gifted child who was fascinated by plate tectonics at age 7 is the same scruffy-faced, trying-to-grow-a-beard son who is now 17 and wishing that school offered more than nature/nurture worksheets. Cherish the relationship you had when your children were younger, and convey today in every way in your power that you still believe in them . . . that you love them . . . that they matter to you, whatever their levels of achievement.

Nuance #2: The Straw Dog of Gender Bias

I am the father of a son and the sole brother of a brother, so my familial connection with girls is limited. Still, something that has long bothered me is the research done by gifted child experts who highlight the unique needs of gifted kids distinctly by gender. After considering the obvious physiological differences between males and females, most cultures make assumptions about each gender in a variety of dimensions: physical strength, emotional makeup, the assumed roles that each gender is likely to play in adulthood, etc. But there is not a culture on Earth where traditional gender roles aren't sometimes ignored or bent by people who just don't buy into them. Girls can become biologists, and boys can become poets; husbands can become stay-at-home dads while their wives make big bucks in the corporate world; boys can cry, and girls can "buck up" and remain stoic. Such role reversals are not always easy and are sometimes ridiculed (or worse) in particular cultures, but generally this blurring of gender identities is practiced and encouraged worldwide.

In reading much of the literature on gifted boys and gifted girls, you are bound to find statements like these (Post, 2015):

- gifted girls lose their interest and passion for learning in middle school, especially in STEM-related subjects;
- gifted girls in middle school lose their confidence and self-esteem; and
- gifted girls are so relational in their interactions with others that they define themselves by gender stereotypes.

And here are a few additional statements, these from the literature related specifically to gifted boys (Minnesota Educators of the Gifted and Talented, 2008):

- gifted boys face societal expectations and pressures that are gender-specific;
- gifted boys frequently have multipotentiality, making it difficult for them to choose a college major or career focus;
- the physiological differences of gifted boys are ignored in school, and their learning styles and preferences are seldom addressed; and
- gifted boys get labeled as troublemakers when they express creativity in the classroom.

Maybe it's me, but if I didn't mention ahead of time which of these statements applied to which gender, my hunch is that you'd have a hard time determining, with one or two exceptions, which ones applied to gifted boys and which to gifted girls. Multipotentiality? Isn't that common with *most* gifted individuals? Losing confidence and self-esteem in middle school? Um . . . that's what puberty does to both sexes. Having your learning styles ignored in school lessons? Name one gifted kid—boy or girl—who hasn't experienced that at one time or another.

My point is that despite cultural expectations to the contrary, we've come a long way in dissolving some of the stereotypes about which gender can do what. Sure, we've got a ways to go (especially with issues like pay equity), but even though it is still more common for a man to be a geologist and a woman to be an elementary teacher, very few fair-minded people scoff at or look askew when a woman studies rocks and a man teaches second grade.

In some areas, what used to be true a generation ago about gifted boys and girls has been turned topsy-turvy. For example, girls now equal or outnumber boys in AP courses, in both the humanities *and* the sciences. Women's college enrollment and graduation rates are also higher than men's. And, if you ask a gifted middle school girl today if she dumbs herself down to look acceptable to the boys, she will likely look at you with puzzlement and say something like, "Hey, if my being smart is a problem for a guy, that doesn't say much about him." Both gifted boys and gifted girls face challenges when it comes to academics and social and emotional issues. Isn't it time to recognize that studying the sexes separately when it comes to these potential challenges is a form of gender bias in and of itself?

I'm afraid that we may have reached the point where gifted boys *and* girls may be having their dreams squashed or redirected in a misbegotten effort to go against their natural inclinations for the sake of gender balance. If a gifted girl opts to become a chemist, she should have every element (excuse the pun) at her disposal to help her reach that goal. However, if a gifted girl's heart lies in becoming a chef, will she be guided against this choice because it's not "gifted" enough? Too, if a gifted boy wants to become a preschool teacher, nurse, or florist, do we send messages, unintentionally or otherwise, that these careers are not quite manly enough?

I do not doubt the well-intentioned efforts of researchers who have chosen to study the topic of gifted girls or boys. In fact, my hunch is that much of the literature produced was written so that capable young people, especially gifted young women, could keep their future options open by selecting high school classes that are rigorous, leaving open many college majors that they would be denied access to without advanced math or science. Still, as I read between the lines of the literature, I note a definite bias. The message seems to be: "Take calculus—it will serve you better than another elective in English." Pretty presumptuous, wouldn't you say? And especially intimidating advice for a gifted young man or woman with a passion for photojournalism rather than photosynthesis.

A high-profile career that is rooted in someone else's dream sustains an individual for only so long. But, when the adolescent dust settles and gifted young adults are left with themselves as the barometers of their personal worth, what a shame it will be if they look back on their careers with more regrets than rewards, realizing that they fulfilled someone else's goals, not their own.

A high-profile career that is rooted in someone else's dream sustains an individual for only so long.

So, as a parent of a gifted boy or girl, be supportive of his or her interests, whether these passions are culturally quirky or typical, and expose him or her to a gender-neutral appreciation of the world. Advocate that your daughter take Tae Kwon Do and your son learn to sew. Bring both your sons and daughters to football games *and* ballets. Don't criticize your daughter's loud belching as unladylike while high-fiving your son on his booming burps. Let your daughter take out the trash while your son does the laundry. Small things add up, and if you react similarly to both your gifted son and gifted daughter who express a desire to become either an astronaut or a kindergarten teacher, then you will be giving them both a timeless and priceless gift: autonomy.

Nuance #3: Personal Fulfillment Through Psychology and Philosophy

When our son was 4 years old, he had a nighttime ritual that forestalled his bedtime by just a few minutes. As we tucked him in, he would inform us how many questions we had to answer before we could leave the bedroom and shut off the light. This good-natured routine was one we all enjoyed, as it put a comfortable capstone on the hectic day of a preschooler.

The questions were typically fanciful ("If Batman and Superman got into a fight, who would win?"), but one night, one particular query stumped us. There would be two questions this evening, Matt told us, so expecting a shorter session than usual, we asked for Question 1. It was an easy answer ("No") to his request to paint his bedroom lime green, so it would look like The Hulk, his favorite superhero. Question 2 was quite different: "Do people feel the same way right before they are born and right after they die?" My wife and I gave one another "the eye," our typical way to indicate "okay . . . you take this one." Except neither of us wanted to take charge here. Finally, as Matt looked at us with a mélange of innocence and wisdom, I took a stab at this philosophical inquiry, "Matt, that's a very good question that people have been asking ever since . . . well, ever since people have been people! I don't know the answer, though, but if I find out, I'll tell you. Is that a deal?"

Matt is now is his 40s and still awaits a response. So do we all.

Sometimes, unknowingly and innocently, our gifted kids can intimidate us by merely being themselves.

In addressing this chapter's third nuance, I thought I'd present some ideas about introducing your gifted children to themselves, from both psychological and philosophical perspectives. Why? Because I've found that many gifted individuals, even the youngest ones, seek answers to questions that either have multiple answers or whose full understanding is based on a set of core beliefs that they might not be able to name, but that are bigger than they are.

For example, I've often heard parents of gifted children talk about their kids as having old souls in young bodies. Not fully content until they have delved into topics that are imaginative, far-fetched, philosophical, and spiritual in nature, these children often probe the wonders of the universe that seem more appropriate for a college seminar than a playground sandbox. They want to know when life began. They want to know if God exists and, if so, "who made God?" They want to reconcile how it can be a crime to kill someone even though many states and nations legally allow the death penalty. They wonder what life would be like for them if they were born a poor child in Guatemala instead of a middle-class kid from Hoboken, and they want to know if there are such things as luck, fate, and whether or not our lives are "programmed" from the minute we're born. They fear death—their own and others'—and they wonder what follows it.

As they announce these questions, often over dinner or while you are driving them home from T-ball practice, you wonder, too. Except what *you* ask yourself is, "I wonder if I am I smart enough to be a good parent to a kid like this?" We don't want to lie to our kids, yet we also don't want to say, "I don't know," so often that it makes us look incompetent. Sometimes, unknowingly and innocently, our gifted kids can intimidate us by merely being themselves.

That's why introducing gifted kids to several topics in psychology and philosophy is helpful, as doing so can help them to put into context some of the nagging thoughts that addle their minds daily. As a parent, you don't have to be a psychologist or philosopher yourself to have valid discussions about big topics; you simply need to combine the information I'll provide here with your own life examples of what these theories and principles look like to you.

Let's begin with a couple of psychological constructs that might be helpful for your gifted child to know about.

Locus of Control (LOC)

Take yourself back to high school. You just took a test in biology class and scored a room-temperature grade of 68%. As you look at these shabby results, which of the following did you say to yourself?

A. "Geez, I really blew this test. I should have studied more than I did."

B. "This just proves what a lousy teacher I have. If he had asked us the right questions, I would have aced this puppy."

If you answered A, then you *internalized* the reason for your lousy grade, taking the blame for not having done your job as a student. If you chose B, you *externalized* this near-failure, blaming someone else for your mediocre performance. In some cases, both A and B could be appropriate responses, but over time and in different academic and social circumstances, people tend to do one on the other: accept responsibility for what goes right or wrong, or shovel the blame or success off to someone else.

This explanation for why things happen as they do in our lives is the crux of the Locus of Control (LOC) construct. First identified decades ago, LOC is subdivided into several categories. Here are two. First, there are people who take full credit for their successes and blame others for anything negative that happens to them. These people are generally annoying to be around, as they fluctuate like the tide between boasting about how smart they are and dismissing as dumb anyone else who doesn't recognize their talents. Conversely, there are individuals who never give themselves justified credit for what they do well, saying things like "I just got lucky" to explain their successes, while internalizing anything that didn't turn out as planned, perhaps stating, "I've never been good at . . . (fill in the blank)." These individuals, too, may not be your favorite dinner companions, as you always leave conversations with them feeling worse than when you started talking to them.

The reason that LOC is an important topic to raise with your gifted children is because it likely impacts their school performance, their willingness to try new things, and their overall self-concept. So, if your internally focused gifted kid buzzed through elementary school without ever studying for a quiz and still earned high grades, she might begin to call herself "dumb" when she finds that things change once she hits middle school, with multiple teachers who have piles of assorted expectations. Too, if your child has an external LOC for trying new things, like a musical instrument or a team sport, he might not even make a meager attempt to begin—because "the teachers and coaches are stupid—they have no clue how talented I am."

The LOC idea has been around for a long time for a reason: It truly impacts how we and our children choose to interact in the world, and it helps to put into context the reasons behind our successes and failures. If you find that your gifted kid is either a little too negative or much too boastful about the reasons things happen as they do, having this psychological tool as a conversation starter is a good way to realign the behavioral balance sheet.

Risk-Taking Versus Risk-Making

Related to LOC, the distinction between risk-taking and risk-making is one I've been touting for years. Here are a couple of scenarios that will help you distinguish between the two.

- **Scenario #1:** Your gifted daughter is a strong math student and has the opportunity to take a college-level trigonometry course in high school. She is reluctant to do so, fearing that it may be way beyond her abilities. As a good, caring parent, you acknowledge her ambivalence, but you say something like, "Your teacher thinks you are capable of doing this, and so do I. Why not give it a try?"

- **Scenario #2:** Your gifted daughter comes home from high school and says, "Guess what: My math teacher has recommended me for a college-level trigonometry class! Isn't that cool! It'll probably be really, really hard, but I can't wait to try!"

Do you notice the distinction? In the first scenario, the overall push to take college-level trigonometry comes from an external source—

you. If your daughter decides to heed your advice, she is *taking* a risk that is being *given to her* by someone else. This is risk-taking. In the second scenario, the person most wanting to take on this challenge is your daughter herself. She is pumped to start something that, inside her psyche, sounds intriguing and challenging. She needs little if any outside encouragement, and in choosing to go her own route, she is *making* a risk of her own design.

Here's why the distinction is vital to understand. If you *take* a risk given by someone else and you succeed, the person affected most by your performance is the individual who challenged you to take this risk in the first place ("See! I knew you could do it!"). And if you don't succeed? Guess what: You, as a kid, feel guilt pangs for not accomplishing what the person who asked you to take the risk assumed you could. On the other hand, if you *make* a risk and you succeed, the first person who pats you on the back is . . . yourself, because you made this risk of your own volition. And if you don't do as well as you'd hoped? The first person you disappoint is also yourself, which is often easier to tolerate than disappointing a mom or dad who has now-dashed hopes for your trigonometric success.

As I stated in a previous publication, "the concept of risk-making actually provides underachievers with a kind of psychological safety, which puts them more in charge of their own destiny than taking a risk from someone else ever could" (Delisle, 2018, p. 40). The magic of distinguishing between risk-taking and risk-making is not limited to underachievers, though. Over many years of teaching and counseling, I have found it to be an equally valuable distinction to draw for even the most successful gifted kids and teens.

Examining Your Life From the Inside Out

Now, let's move on to philosophy . . . with an added element of skateboarding.

The study of philosophy is often seen as an esoteric exercise for deep-thinking, inquisitive adults. And although they certainly are one population that benefits from philosophical discourse, so are gifted kids and their parents who, thanks to a few great resources, now have common ground for investigating life's biggest mysteries and questions.

David White has written several books on how to make philosophy come to life for kids, two of which I'll highlight here: *Philosophy for Kids* (2001) and *The Examined Life: Advanced Philosophy for Kids* (2005). Each book begins with an overview of why philosophy is a topic that is reachable by even young minds. Having worked with students on philosophical topics since 1991, White proposed intricate and interesting ways to incorporate how some seasoned thinkers—Socrates, Seneca, Confucius, Aristotle, Aquinas, Plato—can contribute to such timeless topics as the nature of friendship, the nature of knowledge, and the existence of God. Heavy stuff, to be sure, but through source materials that explain the philosophers' intellectual meanderings, followed by specific and kid-friendly modern applications of philosophy, White put gifted kids, their parents, and teachers on a path to (of course) enlightenment. White then looked at the wisdom provided by more contemporary thinkers like Mother Teresa, Gandhi, and Martin Luther King, Jr., and explained in language that kids can understand, and parents will appreciate, how courageous people practice philosophy through their everyday actions. In *Philosophy for Kids*, White then posed 40 questions that will help readers put into perspective the down-to-Earth application of philosophical stances (e.g., Can something logical not make sense? Can computers think? Who are your friends?).

Are White's books for every gifted kid? Not a chance. But, if you have a 10-year-old who is trying to unravel the mysteries of the universe while his classmates are still trying to master long division, these books are for you. And, never fear, even if you have never taken a philosophy course yourself, these books provide you the tools you need to hold your own, even with your inquisitive gifted kid.

Another way to "go deep," but not as deep as White's work, is to use an activity titled after philosopher John Locke's idea of "tabula rasa"—translated as *blank slate*—that he believed was the mind's condition of each person born into this world. In this activity, which I have used with kids as young as 9, I don't assume that their minds are still blank. On the contrary, I want them to use what they've learned about themselves to complete a series of probing, open-ended statements like these:

- If I could change one thing about my life . . .
- When I consider my future . . .
- I do best in school when . . .
- I do worst in school when . . .
- When I think about my parents . . .
- The most interesting aspect of my life is . . .
- Sometimes I lie awake and night and think . . .
- The most beautiful part of living is . . .
- If I could live one day of my life over again . . .

You get the idea. Each completed statement allows you to probe further into what is important, fun, scary, and hopeful in your gifted child's life. Of course, you should add some of your own statements to these, as should your child. Sometimes, in fact, the ones generated from your own child are the most telling in their depth.

Here is just a sampling from some of my ninth graders who completed the statement, "If I could change one thing about my life . . .":

- I wouldn't be sad anymore.
- I'd want my parents to have the lives they'd dreamed of having when they were young.
- I would spend less time in school.
- I would be taller.

Okay, okay . . . so this last response shows that not all of the answers are deep and meaningful, but even the fun responses can lead to some intriguing conversations, proving that, even though your gifted children may have been *tabula rasas* at birth, they are certainly not blank slates anymore.

One final activity brings us back to the aforementioned skateboarding reference. Here's the story: A former seventh grader of mine, Kenny, was anything but a teacher's dream, academically or behaviorally. But there was something about his writing: Even though it was a grammatical and spelling nightmare, the content was rich and his badly expressed ideas complex. After several conversations with

Kenny, I asked him a pointed, perhaps rude, question: Did he realize that his lack of fundamental writing skills inhibited people from getting the powerful messages that his writing contained? He knew this, of course, attributing it to his dyslexia, which, Kenny said, no one had ever tried to correct. Whether adults failing to help him with his dyslexia is true or not is an open question, but one thing was obvious: When Kenny just talked with me about his big ideas instead of writing them down, I saw in him the excellent thinker that many other teachers did not notice. Over many lunches (and a few detentions), Kenny and I talked about life at its deepest.

Kenny and I parted ways, as teacher and student, at the end of that school year, but a year later, at middle school graduation, Kenny gave me a gift: the then-current issue of *Skateboarder Magazine.* My confused look proved to Kenny that this was not on my typical reading list, but he asked me to turn to the magazine's back page. There I found an interview with a skateboarder in an article titled "Last Words."

"I remembered our talks from last year, Mr. D. I thought you'd like this," Kenny said.

Indeed, I did. For although some of the questions posed in the interview were devoted to skateboarding specifically, others were different, like these:

- When was the last time you lost something?
- When was the last time you felt out of place?
- When was the last time you felt truly happy?
- When was the last time you wanted to give up?
- Who was the last person who inspired you?
- When was the last time you felt loved?

As with the *tabula rasa* activity, feel free to add more "last time" statements as the conversations with your own gifted children grow richer and deeper. One caveat, though: Whatever questions your child answers, you must answer, too. That's only fair, right?

So, the final section of this chapter was devoted to nuance. The beautiful thing about nuance is that it provides lots of intellectual wiggle room. When you have discussions with your gifted children in which you are as active a participant as they are, such interactions often lead to deeper relationships that transcend the roles we all assume in our family units. Talking philosophy with your gifted child may seem like a big task, but, as Robert Browning's famous saying goes, "what's a heaven for?"

Conclusion

Wouldn't it be a lot easier if our gifted kids came complete with instruction books upon their births? Owners' manuals for parents who want to sidestep the stumbles they assume they will make as they lead their able progeny through childhood, adolescence, and into adult independence? Of course, no such volume exists, and even if one did, I hope that no one would buy it. Today parenting is as it has always been—a learn-as-you-go exploration that has no precedent exactly like the situations facing you and your family. There may be some great ideas in parenting books and in friends' and relatives' advice, but when it comes to the specifics of how to best respond to your particular gifted child's quest to know, there are no definitive responses and no guaranteed solutions that will work every time. Instead, parents—just like their gifted kids—are left with nuance. And nuance is good, for it provides time and space for both dialogue and growth.

Today parenting is as it has always been—a learn-as-you-go exploration that has no precedent exactly like the situations facing you and your family.

As a parent, you will be neither flawless nor omniscient, but simply human. This path called parenting is riddled with pitfalls and rocks, yet it is also lined with amazing opportunities to both teach and learn from your child. It all begins by recognizing that imperfection is as inevitable as tomorrow's sunrise and as pervasive as the bright-eyed excitement of a gifted child exploring another new horizon. Your prescription as a parent is defined loosely but well: Be there with a helping hand and a shoulder to lean on. Apply liberally, as needed. Repeat as necessary.

Gifted Children Speak Out

"I am more active in intellectual types of groups and clubs, and for that I am sneered at, called names and looked down at. But I try not to let it get me down because I know the other kids are just jealous, but somehow, this makes it difficult to participate in other activities at school (example: I am always picked last for a softball team in P.E.)."

—Girl, 11, Nebraska

"The worst part of being gifted is the loneliness. I'm from a very small school in a rural area and there aren't many other gifted kids around. I struggle with issues like religion, morality, philosophy and politics, and there simply isn't anyone I can talk to about them. It leads me to feel that I am very, very, very alone in this world. The best part of being gifted is the level of complexity I can comprehend. I love hard concepts that make me reorganize my ways of thinking. Sometimes, when the ideas are coming fast and heavy, it feels like my brain is dancing."

—Boy, 17, Kansas

"My classes are just too easy when it comes to giving us knowledge. We will go over Shay's Rebellion, but we won't discuss how the Rebellion set out a precedent for citizen political expression. We will discuss Sir Isaac Newton, but we will not examine how he influenced not only science, but also music, art, architecture and even literature. I am worried that I will never be stimulated intellectually until college. My older sister says 'it will get harder in high school,' but I am skeptical. When she says 'harder' she means 'more work,' not necessarily intellectually stimulating work.

—Boy, 13, New York

Chapter 7

Deep Roots, Long Branches

Using the Past to Understand the Present

"Before I was married, I had three theories about raising children. Now I have three children and no theories."
—John Wilmot, Earl of Rochester

I'm not sure whether I am more comforted or chagrined that in the more than 300 years since John Wilmot penned those words nothing much has changed! Sure, we have more tools at our disposal than in Wilmot's day. We have psychologists trained to help us understand our children and to help them understand themselves; we have books (like this one) that are intended to assist parents in raising their kids to be happy, fulfilled individuals; and we have pervasive online communities just a mouse click away if we want firsthand advice from other parents confronting what we are facing. Still, all it takes is a quick walk through Wal-Mart where a toddler is screeching to get a "toy twuck," and his two well-educated parents are at wit's end attempting to get the kid under control, to remind us of the wisdom of Wilmot's words. Such is the plight of parenting: Just when we think we have it down, our kids act like kids, and we freeze like the proverbial deer in headlights.

The main reason this occurs, I believe, is that adults have forgotten what they were like as kids—whether they were bratty or submissive, sneaky or out-front honest ("Do you REALLY think brown shoes go with that black suit? Ewww . . ."), parents would do well to recall their own childhood antics. Then, when your gifted kid, who can talk her way out of any punishment due to her facility with words and logic, springs on you what you sprung on *your* parents, you can respond, "I remember trying that line on my parents, Nicole. It's a good one, but it won't work on me."

Whether they were bratty or submissive, sneaky or out-front honest . . . parents would do well to recall their own childhood antics.

But, I digress. The point of this chapter is to remind you that, when it comes to the similarities you share with your children intellectually, the apple doesn't fall far from the tree. Their giftedness came from somewhere and, despite what you might sometimes think, giftedness likely did not skip your generation. Like it or not . . . admit it or not: You have a lot more in common intellectually with your gifted kids than you don't.

In addition to sharing intellectual similarities, parents of gifted kids often share other life elements: intensities, personality traits, and unrealistically high self-expectations. Seldom, though, do adults admit that these and other characteristics might qualify them as gifted. Indeed, denial is rampant: "I might have been gifted as a kid . . ." you will say, but out of fear that someone will think you are inflating your ego, you add quickly, "but I *never* think of myself that way anymore." Then, you change the topic to take the focus off of yourself. If this response is something that you either have said or would say, know that the message it sends to your gifted child is this: "I want you to be proud of your giftedness, even as I am dismissing my own."

The Research on Gifted Adults Says . . .

I've long been leery of research in education and psychology that seems to be conducted to prove a point the researcher believed in the first place. Of course, some studies are well-designed and their results generalizable to a larger population of people, but then, there are many "well, duh!" studies, such as those highlighted by *Entrepreneur Magazine* as the dumbest research studies of each year (Marks, 2016). Among the 2016 winners were these: One study that was done at Cambridge University, mockingly referred to as "Spiderman doesn't exist," discovered that the larger a person is, the more adhesives he would need to stick to a wall. Another study at McGill University proved (yes, *proved*) that world-class athletes have stronger legs and 14% more muscle than sedentary adults of the same age. These less-than-Earth-shattering results lead my sometimes-jaded self to conclude that "educational research" is often an oxymoron.

When I consider some of the research related to gifted individuals, the same metric is true: Some of it is relevant and meaningful, but other studies should probably never have been done in the first place. Still, some research on gifted individuals has stood the test of time, such as the work of Lewis Terman and Leta Hollingworth in the early 1900s. Among their findings was this nugget of news: Parents of gifted kids and their children very often have similar IQs (Terman, 1925). Now, I realize that IQ does not tell the full story about gifted-ness, but it is a time-tested technique for measuring the mind, so let's not discount its many merits, even while recognizing its limitations.

As Terman and others focused on quantitative research to draw their conclusions about gifted children, other individuals looked at evidence that was less driven by numbers and statistics, and more focused on the lived experiences of gifted children and their parents. This type of research is called *qualitative*, not quantitative, and it relies on observations over time, utilizing both one's expertise and experience to put these observations into context. Annemarie Roeper, whose work I mentioned earlier, was an expert at qualitative analysis, using her decades of work with gifted children and adults to pinpoint a variety of characteristics and emotions that link parents of gifted children with similar characteristics and emotions in their gifted kids.

In her 60+ years of experience working with gifted individuals of all ages, Roeper discovered that many gifted adults didn't believe they qualified as such because they didn't change the world in noteworthy ways—they didn't invent new theorems, paint any masterpieces, or bring about world peace. By equating giftedness with outstanding accomplishments, many gifted adults saw themselves as nothing special at all. But Roeper (1995) disagreed:

> The greatest impact is actually made by the vast majority of the gifted whose light does not shine on the universe, but instead penetrates our daily lives. These are the gifted teachers, parents, cooks, bus drivers and letter writers. They are the quietly gifted—the privately gifted. Most often they're not aware of their giftedness. But the same characteristics are found in the privately gifted as in those whose contributions are better known. (p. 94)

Roeper (1995) then went on to uncover 23 different characteristics she had seen impact the lives of gifted adults, all of which are listed in Figure 3, and some of which are elaborated on further in this chapter. Her main point was this:

> Giftedness is an ongoing process and not a product. The process leads in a direction that differs from the direction of the majority, but which can also integrate with it and bring about change. It can lead to the greatest wretchedness and the highest ecstasy. The gifted person has the capacity to penetrate the complexities of the landscape of life and understand its supreme interconnectedness. Experiencing one's own giftedness—one's creative abilities—is one of the most exciting aspects of the gifted person's life. (p. 107)

Characteristics and Emotions of Gifted Adults

1. Gifted adults differ intellectually from others.
2. Gifted adults retain childlike emotions.
3. Gifted adults often feel fundamentally different about themselves than others feel about them.
4. Gifted adults are often driven by their giftedness.
5. Gifted adults may be overwhelmed by the pressure of their own creativity.
6. Gifted adults often have strong feelings encompassing many areas of life.
7. Gifted adults are not necessarily popular.
8. Gifted adults need solitude and time for contemplation and daydreaming.
9. Gifted adults search for meaning in both the inner world and the outer world.
10. Gifted adults often develop their own method of learning and grasping concepts.
11. Gifted adults have a special problem awareness.
12. Gifted adults are able to see patterns of development and growth, and therefore will recognize trends.
13. Gifted adults often react angrily to being subjected to public relations methods of image making.
14. Gifted adults are perfectionists.
15. Gifted adults are often confronted with the problem of having too many abilities in too many areas in which they would like to work, discover, and excel.
16. Gifted adults often have feelings of being misunderstood, of being outsiders, and of being unable to communicate.
17. Gifted adults have difficulty understanding the seemingly inconsistent and shortsighted behavior of others.
18. Gifted adults perceive a difference between justice and equality.
19. Gifted adults may find it more difficult than others to take risks because they realize more what is at stake.
20. One of the most outstanding features of gifted adults is their sense of humor.
21. Gifted adults can develop emotional problems related to their abilities, but they also have greater resources for dealing with their problems.
22. Gifted adults often have difficulty with authority figures.
23. Many gifted people have strong moral convictions and try to use their specific talents, insights, and knowledge for the betterment of the world.

FIGURE 3. Characteristics and emotions of gifted adults. Adapted from Roeper, 1995, pp. 93–108.

As you read this passage, you probably thought about the gifted child you are raising. And, if truth be told, you should probably reconcile the fact that this statement applies equally to you, the parent.

Let's examine several of the statements in Figure 3 in more depth, remaining conscious of the connection between the traits you see in your gifted child and those you see in yourself.

1. *Gifted adults differ intellectually from others.* More conceptual than piecemeal in their thinking, gifted adults grasp difficult concepts and phenomena that others struggle to decipher. Resentment can set in when you try to get others to see things as the complexities that they are, only to be told that you are too much: too abstract, too elaborate, too radical, too . . . everything. Trying to convince others of the merits of your ideas often proves futile, because the skies you see are not the skies they observe.

2. *Gifted adults retain childlike emotions.* A delight in new discoveries or insights can make you giddy, and you internalize to a deep degree the pains that others would brush off. Dismissed as either naïve or immature, you are simply expressing the honest emotions that are a part of your being. Michael Piechowski (2006) recorded this observation from a 16-year-old girl struggling to keep balance with her emotions:

> When I was younger, either I liked the mood around me or I shut myself away from it. Right now I feel like a puppet in constant struggle to cut its own strings. I don't want how I feel to depend on others, and yet I don't want to shut them out anymore. (p. 141)

6. *Gifted adults may have strong feelings encompassing many areas of life.* When you hear about the intensities and overexcitabilities possessed by gifted individuals, two things come to mind: First, you recognize that you could be the poster child for these traits, and second, you cringe at the realization that you have been "outed." Everything matters . . . and it matters that it matters. When (or if) you find someone who has similar intensities, your whole world can change, as the

sense of isolation that often accompanies such strong feelings is cauterized—your emotional bleeding has been halted.

9. *Gifted adults search for meaning in both the inner world and the outer world.* Making money and having a nice house is good—but not good enough. The gifted adult strives to construct a life full of purpose and is sometimes frustrated when others do not share this philanthropic vision of what could be. Yet, through bettering the lives of others, this person—you—becomes more whole. Others may scoff at your "pie in the sky" thinking or your misplaced optimism in a world filled with strife, but your enthusiastic embrace of a tomorrow better than today catapults you into the realm of the possible.

16. *Gifted adults often have feelings of being misunderstood, of being outsiders, and of being unable to communicate.* Roeper (1995) considered this situation to be the most difficult problem facing gifted individuals. In response, many gifted adults create in isolation—penning poetry they do not share or exploring esoteric hobbies that others just wouldn't understand. The result can be enriching, lonely, or both. To cite (again) the words and wisdom of Leta Hollingworth (1942), "Isolation is the refuge of genius, not its goal" (p. 167); but when sharing your passions with others results in rolled eyes or behind-your-back snickers, such isolation might feel safer than revelation.

18. *Gifted adults perceive a difference between justice and equality.* Too many people consider *equality* and *sameness* to be synonyms, but gifted people do not. Gifted adults can justify doling out different rewards for the same success or different punishments for the same crime; it will depend on the person and the circumstances, as relativity trumps blind dogma. Although others perceive this as inconsistency or favoritism, gifted adults merely see it as logical. As you might imagine, gifted adults' favorite color is gray.

19. *Gifted adults may find it more difficult than others to take risks because they realize more what is at stake.* The risk might be physical, intellectual, or emotional, and before taking the plunge, gifted adults consider—sometimes overly so—the consequences of their behavior. As Roeper (1995) wrote, "It will take the gifted longer to decide to dive into the pool, but they will be less likely to hit their heads on the bottom" (p. 106). The distinction I brought up earlier between

risk-taking and risk-making applies to gifted adults, not just children. One difference, though, is that a gifted adult, once burned by the unrelenting fire of other people's opinions, may be less likely to even chance being honest for fear of being misunderstood.

21. *Gifted adults can develop emotional problems related to their abilities, but they also have greater resources for dealing with their problems.* Although gifted adults are often hardest on themselves when it comes to meeting self-set expectations, questioning whether they are really as smart as everyone says they are, they also have a greater capacity than others to step back and look at their situations rationally. Over time, this brings both comfort and satisfaction to them. Once their own worst enemies, they can become their own best friends.

The knowledge of characteristics of gifted adults is encapsulated in the work of Roeper (1995), but she is not alone in recognizing these lifelong attributes. In *Searching for Meaning: Idealism, Bright Minds, Disillusionment, and Hope*, distinguished psychologist James Webb (2013) addressed how gifted adults can cope—indeed, *thrive*—by learning strategies that help them transcend the negative or parochial views of others. Perhaps Webb said it best in the book's dedication to Dr. Llewellyn Queener, calling him "a caring professor who patiently helped and guided me when my thinking hurt too much" (p. v). Also, Ellen Fiedler (2015), in her book *Bright Adults: Uniqueness and Belonging across the Lifespan*, used a sailing metaphor to guide gifted adults through journeys and paths mapped out eons ago by ancient seagoing searchers. In doing so, Fiedler offered advice for gifted adults to remain authentic to their ideals, to contribute to their world, and to find challenge continually in their lives. And then, of course, there is the elegant work of Michael Piechowski, who brought emotional comfort to gifted adults who possess overexcitabilities that others often can't fathom. According to Piechowski and Daniels (2008), because gifted adults are criticized by people who do not understand that these traits are as natural as their eye color or height, gifted adults learn to disguise or suppress the very traits that make them exceptional. The danger in doing so is this: If you happen to have lived life as a gifted child whose intensities were neither appreciated nor tolerated, you may now, as a parent, try to shelter your gifted child from the isolation you may have felt growing up. This is a natural tendency—to protect those we love. Still, it does your children a disservice to ignore these overexcitabilities or to downplay their pervasiveness in a gifted individual's life. So, if you see your children exhibiting many of the traits and heightened emotions that are part and parcel of growing up gifted, you need to discuss the beauty that can be derived from seeing in vivid clarity a world that others see through limited, opaque lenses.

I can't end this section on gifted adults without returning to the original source one more time: the wisdom of Annemarie Roeper. At the age of 90, Roeper (2011) compiled a set of essays about growing old as a gifted person. Yes, she was still an adult, but now, nearing the end of her life, she questioned why others saw her frail body and assumed that she also had a frail mind. Trust me . . . she did not. In *Beyond Old Age: Essays on Living and Dying*, Roeper explored what it means to be a gifted elder in a world that prizes youth so avidly. Reflecting on both her past and her present, Roeper wrote this:

> In a long life like mine you begin to think that nothing new could ever happen again, and yet I know that the greatest unpredictability is still ahead of me. . . . Is there a God? Is there a guiding force? . . . We need to have faith in that mystery. That alone may be the greatest wisdom the world has to offer us. (pp. 11–13)

How wonderful a message! Roeper did not tell us what to think or believe; she merely wanted us to consider all of our life options. Indeed, Roeper's greatest legacy to the gifted field was her belief that gifted children, once grown into adulthood and old age, are as valuable and unique as the gifted children they once were.

A Note About Depression

In reading the previous section of this chapter, you may be wondering if gifted children and adults who experience life in such a high emotional key are more prone to mental illnesses and addictions than the general population. After all, if gifted individuals feel as alone as Roeper (1995) noted that they often do, isn't depression more likely to occur? And, if the world as it exists leaves you feeling hollow inside, isn't it preferable to carve out a new, artificial one with any manner of substances that create a new reality that is less bleak or more fanciful? Too, should all of the drugs in the world fail to upgrade your self-image as someone who matters, does suicide become a viable option for the gifted, lonely person?

These issues have been researched some, but not so much that any definitive conclusions can be drawn. Although there is no empirical evidence that gifted individuals are more likely to suffer from clinical depression or to abuse prescription or illegal drugs than the general population (Neihart, Pfeiffer, & Cross, 2015; Webb et al., 2016), anecdotal evidence is abundant that being gifted does not make one *immune* from mental illness. Early on in the study of giftedness (or "genius," as it was called way-back-when), a "scientist" named Cesare Lombroso (1893) thought that insanity and genius were bedfellows; based on Lombroso's "logic," every individual is born with a certain amount of brainpower that, once exhausted, leaves him or her mentally incapacitated to function as he or she once did. Therefore, because geniuses think more quickly and strongly than others, Lombroso postulated that they become insane in rather short order, as their "mind muscles" are spent.

Fortunately, when Lewis Terman came around in the 1920s, he determined that the 1,528 young people identified for his longitudinal study, *Genetic Studies of Genius* (Terman, 1925), were as mentally healthy, or more so, than the general population. This finding extended into the adult lives of Terman's subjects, crushing Lombroso's ideas into much pseudoscientific chalk dust. However, the legacy Terman left behind was mixed; now that he had shown that gifted individuals were a fundamentally healthy lot, physically and emotionally, the impression was left that gifted people could act upon any crisis of confidence independent of others' assistance. In just one generation, gifted people went from being creatures of emotional fragility to paragons of mental health. Truth be told, neither extreme is accurate.

Today, remnants of both Terman's and Lombroso's ideas remain part of the mythological fabric about the makeup of gifted individuals. For just as there are some who consider the gifted to be "a little off . . . a little weird," there are others who contend that the gifted need no special assistance in school or life, because "they are so smart they can make it on their own." The first impression is left over from the dark days of Lombroso, while the latter is a naïve interpretation of Terman's findings on the relative strength of gifted individuals' psyches.

The truth lies where it usually does—somewhere in the middle. So, just as I can state unequivocally that there is little evidence to prove that gifted individuals are more fragile than most when it comes to affairs of the heart and mind, I can also state unequivocally that there is little evidence that they are more able than others to handle life's emotional speed bumps without psychological injuries.

However, when depression does occur in gifted children and adults, it is often colored in a slightly different shade of blue than in the general population. Webb (2013) used the term "existential depression" to describe life situations where gifted individuals feel alienated, psychologically empty, and alone, because "their high intellect allows them to contemplate the cosmos and their very small place in it" (p. 80). They realize that life is a temporary condition, that there is no conclusive meaning to the purpose of individual lives, and that personal meaning is often not valued by the individuals most present in their day-to-day interactions. Tied in directly with the individual's personal qualities that make him or her gifted in the first place—the ability to think at higher levels, to make connections between disparate concepts and events, to envision a world that others his or her own age (or older) do not see—existential depression can take up residence in the child's soul, not just the gifted adult's. Should this happen, the internal loneliness is palpable and often painful.

Existential depression may show itself in a number of ways:

- A pessimistic attitude about life that "the worst is yet to come." Every cloud has a lining, but it is seldom silver.
- Antisocial, negative behaviors that show up in sulkiness, aggression, rudeness, school conduct problems, and impatience with others. The true inner hurt is disguised by these

outward displays, often misinterpreted as anger instead of elements of depression.

- A forlorn sense that one's life cannot make a difference in a world beset with problems that even intelligent people refuse to act upon.
- A feeling of being overwhelmed by the number of possibilities open to gifted individuals in terms of future occupations. This feeling can result in a resignation that "I don't have enough time to do it all," causing a feeling of hollow success even with strong achievement.
- A feeling of rejection or separation from other children and adults who do not see the realities you do and, therefore, marginalize your anxieties as unimportant.

Existential depression does not occur just because a gifted person thinks about the enormity of life, the inequities obvious in a complex world of billions of people, one's personal future, or the status of our planet's health. Existential depression *does* begin to appear when the gifted child's or teen's views of reality are dismissed or demeaned by others. If the gifted child feels that there is no one to talk to, to share fears and solutions, or to simply cry out in anger or frustration, the seeds for existential depression are sown. This feeling of psychic isolation is bad enough when the child's classmates regard these concerns as trivial, but the trouble really begins when adults react in ways that suggest a gifted child's grasp of reality is loose. Some gifted kids might expect their classmates to be clueless about the wider world, but when adults who are supposed to know better are oblivious to the very real concerns that the gifted child expresses, then where is that child to turn? The answer? No place good.

So, what are you to do, as the parent of a gifted child showing signs of existential depression? First, you need to take a breath and realize that your child is likely not saying what she is saying in order to scare you or get your attention. What she is sharing comes from a need to know that is simply a part of being able to see so clearly what others her age may not even perceive. Recheck those characteristics of gifted children and the qualities of gifted adults mentioned by Piechowski

(2006, 2014), Roeper (1995), and others in this book, and you will note the source of this angst.

Second, be ready to listen. Do not provide pat answers that both you and your child know are lame and only meant to make her feel better. So, instead of saying, "I'm sure many people in our government are working on ways to eliminate childhood poverty," say this: "Sometimes, our government seems to have its priorities screwed up. Very few people your age realize this, but you see it clearly." A statement like this supports your child's view of reality and, if nothing else, continues the conversation for one more day.

Third, share any similar frustrations that you might have. A statement like, "I'd like to let you know about a situation that has been bothering me that I think you will understand. Can I share it with you?" can open doors to communication that have previously been shut. Such a statement/request implies that you value your child's opinion. Even more, though, it shows a degree of trust and openness that is not a universal hallmark of parent-child relationships. Most importantly, it conveys an unspoken but vital message: "You are not alone in your frustrations or anxiety."

Lastly, allow your child to propose a solution that might address even a small part of the issue being raised. At times, problems—be they global or personal—seem so big because the solutions to them seem so distant. But, even putting a tiny dent in energy depletion by walking to work one day a week, or saying to one friend who has dissed your ideas, "When you laughed at my concern about bullying at school, I felt hurt. I just wanted you to know that," may release some of the pressure built up by having no one to talk to but oneself. Giving gifted kids a voice, and encouraging them to share it, may not always work to their advantage, but they need to know that, from your perspective, their voice is valued and worth hearing.

Bottom line: You can take a *mess* and turn it into a *message* by opening the doors of communication with your gifted children and letting them in on the sweet little secret shared in this chapter: that gifted children grow up to be gifted adults. The questions that gifted 5-year-olds contemplate about the universe and its mysteries are thoughts that will follow them throughout their lives. With understanding and guidance, your presence along the way may not eliminate existential depression entirely, but it will put depression into proper perspective when it eventually does appear. Lead with your heart; it won't steer you wrong.

On Crossing Bridges Prematurely: Zeb's Heart

The end of each chapter in this book contains reflections from children about some aspect of growing up gifted, yet it only seemed right that this chapter highlighting the characteristics of gifted adults should contain insights from an adult. So, I present Zebulon, a 26-year-old gifted adult who both struggled with and embraced the emotional ups and downs he experienced since he was a boy. I met Zebulon—Zeb—when he was a seventh grader, a student in my middle school gifted program. Zeb called our gifted class his "sanctuary," as it was the only place in school that he was allowed to be fully himself.

Zeb and I continued our relationship throughout his high school and college years, and we still keep in touch today. Now a married man with a career as a military officer, Zeb maintains the same closeness to his emotions that I came to know and admire when he was on the cusp of entering adolescence. Several years ago, I asked Zeb if he would write an essay on what it was like to be him growing up. He gladly obliged and, in true Zeb form, wrote a piece that, to this day, brings tears to my eyes.

Using a powerful metaphor, Zeb compared his emotions to that of a hurricane, a huge, swirling, tumultuous storm that, at its eye, contains a small area of calm. Here is how Zeb explained it:

> There is such a high level of intensity, but inside of it all, I can find a tiny place where I feel completely comfortable. All this emotion is useful in that I find it easy to be sympathetic to my friends' problems . . . but other times, it becomes burdensome. (Galbraith and Delisle, 2011, p. 72)

Zeb then went on to explain how he has *always* been able to get to the core of emotions with people of all ages and, although his classmates mostly appreciated his caring intervention, adults sometimes didn't. Zeb continued:

A much younger I, around age 12, picked up (by observation) that an adult in my life was lonely. She didn't act like it or pine publicly, but I saw in her kind face that she had something missing. While talking to her, I mentioned that a cousin of mine was living alone, and that she said it was lonely. I asked her if she was lonely. She became upset with me, and told me that it was rude to say things like that. I know now why she became upset. A 12-year-old told her what she was trying to ignore herself. She *was* lonely. But I never brought the issue up again. (Galbraith and Delisle, 2011, pp. 72–73)

Struck down for not "knowing his place" with adults, Zeb was able to put this harsh adult reaction into the mature perspective he possessed that belied his youth. He concluded his essay with a long-view, philosophical analysis on the benefits and drawbacks of being himself:

Life is a series of important emotional events and revelations. I know that I have come upon a great deal of these early in my life. Sometimes I think I'd be better off without the depth of understanding that I have, but I always come around to knowing that it is my capacity to understand and see what others don't that makes me the person I am. And I wouldn't trade that for anything. (p. 73)

In the concluding section of her book, *Bright Adults: Uniqueness and Belonging Across the Lifespan*, Ellen D. Fiedler (2015) mentioned that "solo sailors often report that they feel as if they 'find themselves' when sailing alone" (p. 214). How true is this, do you think, for young gifted adults like Zeb, who navigate the waters of human interactions with unexpected maturity?

But even solo sailors need wind at their backs if they are to avoid the stifling doldrums that can prompt loneliness and despair. Solo sailors also need a home port, someplace safe and secure where they know they can always return. Too, solo sailors may cross open waters by themselves, but the architects who helped to construct their ship and the cartographers who guided them with detailed maps are very much a part of the solo sailor's success.

As the caring individual who is hoping for clear sailing and calm waters for your own solo sailors, know that the role you play in helping them chart their courses is a vital ingredient to their own success. A magazine editor and accomplished seaman, Howard Bloomfield, said that "cruising the open seas has two main pleasures: One is to go out into wider waters from a sheltered place. The other is to go into a sheltered place from wide waters" (as cited in Fiedler, 2015). In both situations, your guidance and experience will serve your solo sailors well.

Are You Smarter Than Your Fifth Grader?

Call me a curmudgeon if you want to, but I'm not a fan of reality television shows, especially those whose main point seems to be making contestants look silly or stupid—sometimes both. One particularly offensive entry into the reality show world of debasement was *Are You Smarter Than a 5th Grader?* hosted by jokester Jeff Foxworthy. On it, kids were pitted against adults to see who could answer trivia questions that have little bearing on one's actual level of intelligence. Of course, it was more fun when the adult contestants looked dumb and belittled, but I found the whole enterprise disheartening. Why? Capable adults were made to look stupid, and smart kids were getting acknowledged exclusively for their ability to *make* the adults look dumb. Yawn . . .

Another more serious reason why I don't appreciate such displays of trivial intelligence is because there is a common anxiety shared by many parents of gifted kids that they are not smart enough to raise their own gifted kids. Shows like *Are You Smarter Than a 5th Grader?* bring those deep-seated fears to the surface. I've raised this issue earlier in my book—feeling inadequately "smart" as a parent to raise your gifted kid—but it's worth repeating here.

Fearing the worst if you make a mistake, like not allowing your gifted 4-year-old to enter kindergarten early (or, for that matter, *allowing* your child to enter early despite the express objections of school personnel), you second-guess every decision of consequence. You lose sleep over whether you did the right thing by forcing your son to take piano lessons that he'd rather avoid, or making your daughter join the youth soccer league even though she has no interest whatsoever in team sports. You may even avoid helping with homework or school projects, fearing that you will give the wrong answer or advice, resulting in a child who is scarred for life due to your intellectual oafishness.

My advice to you if you feel these anxieties? Relax your mind and turn off reality TV shows that pinpoint how inadequate you are. Then, substitute *this* slice of reality: Like every parent, you will eventually reach a point where helping your child with an assignment seems purposeless, as the content is either foreign to you or too complex. With gifted kids, this may occur early, in fifth or sixth grade, not when you expected it might occur, like in the college-level calculus class your daughter is taking during her senior year of high school. As parents, we are prepared for our children to outshine us academically at some point, but when this takes place before kids hit puberty, many parents of gifted kids seek cover behind closed doors in fear of hearing that intimidating question, "Mom, can you help me with this?"

If you have these anxious feelings, the best way to address them is to let your gifted kids in on a secret—*you don't know everything*. Of course, when you share this truth, your kids will probably look at you with one of those eye-rolling glares that let you know you've just stated the obvious. Remember, except for the very youngest gifted kids, our kids have learned from past experience that even though you may want to help with their homework, you can't always do so. They may humor you and say, "Thanks for your help," as they wend their way back to their studies, but just admitting the obvious—that you don't know how to help with some of their schoolwork—is better than faking it, providing academic guidance in a subject you have not studied (or cared about) for the last 20 years. A simple "I don't have the answer to that" is preferable to a wrong answer in a subject in which you are not conversant.

You are more approachable as a parent if you are not a know-it-all. . . . Imperfect role models are easier to emulate than perfect ones.

The good thing is that your gifted kid probably doesn't care very much that you are not a walking, talking search engine with answers to every query. Instead, your kids want to see you the way they see themselves—imperfect and vulnerable. Think of it—you are more approachable as a parent if you are not a know-it-all. Admitting that some topics are difficult or answers elusive for you validates your child's perception that life and learning have some limitations. Too, if you find a subject or issue difficult that they are also struggling with, this connects you in ways that false omniscience does not. You become more human when you share your ignorance about at least some things that exist in this complex world we all inhabit. Imperfect role models are easier to emulate than perfect ones.

But simply saying, "I don't know," to your gifted kids' questions does not get you off the hook. As a parent, you can provide a different type of guidance by doing something unexpected, like the following:

- Sit down with your child (or by yourself) and do a little research that may help to better answer his or her questions. Let your child's responsiveness to this assistance guide you; 10 minutes may be sufficient, or 2 hours may not be long enough.
- If you know someone conversant in a field of interest to your child, ask if that person has any advice, knowledge, or resources that might be helpful for your child. You could ask your child to do this, but your initiative in doing so sends a positive message that you heard your child's request and you took it upon yourself to probe further into finding solutions you could not provide right away.
- There will be times when it is not the content of a child's task that is confusing as much as it is the scope of the project itself.

An independent study on World War II is a bit, shall we say, daunting without some specific parameters as to the particular focus of the study. Everything from D-Day planning, to Japanese internment camps, to the role Russia played in an Allied victory is worthy of a book unto itself. Your job? To help your child determine what bite-size pieces can be explored.

- Follow up. If your child asks for your assistance and you give what you know, wait a couple of days and ask how the project is going. If you were not able to be of much help directly, you can still show your support by inquiring about the status of the assignment. Or, when your child completes the project, ask her if she wants you to look it over, and if she would like you to check it for content, style, or clarity. Your role as a critic will be received better if your gifted kid has told you specifically what to look for as you read.

The role you play as a parent of a gifted child is complex beyond belief, and the times when you are probably needed most are those when it appears your child wants you there the least, like in early adolescence. So ask yourself these questions: Can you be supportive, yet not obtrusive? Interested, but not cloying? Inquisitive, but not nosy? If you can answer "yes" to these questions, my guess is that the communication between you and your gifted child will allow you to see each other as allies in the learning process.

Conclusion

It's something of a paradox, this thing called giftedness. As smart as they are, gifted kids can feel dumb when confronted by life's inevitable mistakes and challenges. As logical as they appear, they may be at the loosest of ends when trying to decipher how a long-standing friendship went awry. And, as multitalented as they might be, it becomes a struggle to home in on those one or two areas that would satisfy their curiosity in a career or college major.

Parents of gifted kids, too, can seem rather contradictory. You want your gifted children to be proud of their abilities, but when they ask how you are gifted, you cringe and blush, and avoid the question more often than you answer it. You understand that giftedness encompasses heightened emotions and rich cognitive processing, yet when you show your feelings and intellect with full intensity, you look around to make sure no one is watching. You tell your kids it's okay to make mistakes, yet when you mess up in a big way, you do everything you can to clean it up before anyone else notices—after all, "a smart person like you should know better."

The intent of this chapter was to show you your own mirror image—the gifted child you are raising and how similar he or she is to you. Some parents of gifted kids will deny that their children got their brains through genetics, but it is my hope that you will take a straightforward look at yourself to find that the intellectual and emotional overlap you share with your gifted children is real and strong. As a gifted adult, you need to acknowledge the similarities you have with your gifted children. Then, when the occasions arise and the conversations flow smoothly, talk about some of your hopes and anxieties with that son or daughter who is seeking the same answers you do about life's biggest questions. Finally, see yourself in a position that parents often play, yet seldom acknowledge: the emotional role model who may not have all of the answers, but who is bowled over continually by the possibilities that lie ahead.

Gifted Children Speak Out

"There is some correlation between age and maturity, but not really all that much. Just as I am realizing that 16 is an artificial age of maturity that I have created for myself, the age of 18 or 21 is just as artificial. It is an expiration date that the government has placed on all our childhoods, and it is just as exact as those placed by the FDA. Nothing horrible will happen to toothpaste if it sits on the shelf too long, but the FDA has determined that there is a higher chance it will be ineffective if it is over such an age. The same strategy is used for determining the age of maturity, only in reverse. It is a horrible, inexact method of determining maturity, as book and moral learning are quite separate."

—Girl, 15, Pennsylvania

"My parents often say, 'Don't embarrass us by turning into some sort of bookworm. Play sports, get dirty outside, and enjoy yourself. There will be plenty of time to test out and exercise that brain of yours in your life.'"

—Boy, 15, Alaska

"My parents are always talking about me being gifted and how different I am compared to other people my age. They tell me how lucky I am to be smart and that I should never be ashamed of myself or anything I do. They expect my grades to be in the 90s, and they also expect me to do the right thing when I go to places like parties or movies."

—Boy, 14, Texas

Chapter 8

Write Your Dreams in Pencil

"Cheshire Puss," [said Alice]. . . . "Would you tell me, please, which way I ought to go from here?"

"That depends a good deal on where you want to get to," said the Cat.

"I don't care much where—" said Alice.

"Then it doesn't matter which way you go," said the Cat.

"—so long as I get somewhere," Alice added as an explanation.

"Oh, you're sure to do that," said the Cat, "if only you walk long enough."

—Lewis Carroll, *Alice's Adventures in Wonderland*

B oulder, CO: sun-splashed vistas of the Flatiron mountain peaks, streams gurgling through the middle of town, "trustafarians" (rich kids who dress like abandoned waifs) donned in tie-dye on Pearl Street. Indeed, western atmospherics at their finest. Oh yes, there is also the University of Colorado Boulder (CU), as beautiful a college campus setting as you will find anywhere. It was that university that our son, Matt, at age 12 said he wanted to attend.

Knowing Matt, we didn't argue, for we knew that he changed his mind about future matters as frequently as I changed my socks. We decided to embrace his interest in CU, occasionally asking questions about why he wanted to attend there, what attracted him to a region of the country he had visited only twice, and what CU offered in terms of interesting majors that intrigued him. Matt's answer to our queries about CU's academics was always the same: "I don't care about 'majors' . . . I just want to *ski*!"

Oh well, when you're 12 years old, I guess there could be worse reasons for wanting to move to Colorado!

But, his yen for CU never wavered. Year after year, Matt's fascination with this campus in the West increased. From our Ohio home, he watched every football game he could find on ESPN where the CU Buffaloes were involved, and each winter, Matt tallied the length of the ski season, the frequency that I-70 was closed at Vail Pass, and the number of inches of snow that had fallen throughout the long, long winters. But his initial interest in Colorado skiing grew into seriousness as he began to contemplate academic majors and, upon finding that CU offered his chosen field of study, film, Matt locked in with surety that he would soon be a Buffalo.

So, when it came time to apply to college, Matt chose CU. Even knowing full well that his acceptance was not assured, he did what any aspiring, optimistic teenager would do—he applied for early admission, informing us that he was not applying elsewhere.

"I'll get in," he told us with indomitable surety.

We gulped in fear that our son, a strong student with a good, though not stellar, high school record, would not land the dream he had chosen to target. The University of Colorado has high admission standards and receives applications from thousands of Buffalo wannabes. Would Matt pass the muster and be seen by the admissions staff in the same way we saw our son—as an independent, focused, intelligent, and sensitive dreamer filled with passion and determination?

To make a long story short, CU said yes! As I came home that glorious day of college acceptance, with Matt sitting at the kitchen table among a pile of forms, he looked up and uttered seven words through tear-streaked eyes: "Dad, I'm going to be a Buffalo!"

His dream realized, the serious matters of choosing a dorm, applying for scholarships, and making plans for the big move west occupied Matt's full attention. As his parents, we just sat back and watched, helping when he asked, awash in the glow of our son's excitement and proud of the sense of purpose that accompanied Matt's sense of moving forward into an unknown future.

Arriving in Boulder in late August, Matt didn't even grit his teeth (we did) when we saw that his dorm room overlooked a dumpster, not the mountains. And he didn't seem alarmed (we did) when his roommate, a guy from Florida, was already on academic probation due to low grades and some unexplained "police involvement" during his required summer classes. Matt didn't even seem concerned (we did) when he learned that his survey class in chemistry would have more than 400 students in its lecture section—about half the size of his entire high school.

But ah . . . there were the mountains that he couldn't quite see, and the promise of crisp, autumn afternoons at football games. And there would be classes that Matt would enjoy and be challenged in, and the chance to make new friends and cavort with them over pizza at *The Sink* restaurant. Also, if all else failed, some good friends of ours lived only 60 minutes away, where a home-cooked meal and familiar voices would gloss over any homesickness that might occur. The stage was set for a perfect melding of dream with reality.

Until this:

September 16

Dear Mom and Dad:

At present, a desire to quell many of my anxieties, fears and stresses that reside inside of me causes me to write to you. During the past several days, I have found that I am continually contemplating the "what ifs" of my future. I know I am not alone in my fears, but still, that doesn't ease my worried mind. It seems that college and all that surrounds its demands are too overwhelming. I find myself studying continually, but still feeling that I am looking up a long ladder even after closing my textbooks. However, as I walk to and from class or the library, I see a large abundance of students enjoying themselves in the various courtyards and fields that the University grounds contain. As I watch and listen to the smiles and laughter coming from their direction, I ask myself what I am doing wrong to deny myself such luxuries and happiness.

Another concern I have had in recent weeks is my longing to live in the past—the innocence and pleasure of childhood are thoughts I hope never escape my mind. I find myself remembering how much I enjoyed childhood, and I want above all else to be a third or fourth or sixth grader again. There is a strong feeling inside of me that the past hurried along too quickly and that the future is all too near. Does such thinking suggest that I have grown up? I would certainly hope not. Does such thinking raise questions of my maturity, my ability to adapt to change? I would like to think that most people, at similar points in their development, raise these same questions inside of their minds, as they struggle to survive during the darkness that haunts them each evening.

What can I do regarding all of these fears, anxieties and questions? I was hoping in writing to you that you could assure me that I am thinking "normally" as most people under stress think.

Love,
Matt

There . . . did you see it? Did you catch the unstated yet obvious message? That the evaporation of Matt's dream was happening right in front of our eyes?

Our son's freshman year in college was the worst one we ever experienced as parents. Even daily talks with Matt did not help bridge the 1,200-mile gap that separated us, and home-cooked meals from our family friends were appreciated but not sufficient to bolster Matt once he returned to a lonely campus. As the fall semester passed, even the upcoming ski season didn't add spark to the unfocused disillusionment that, once present, never left our son's being. We couldn't wait for him to return home in December; he couldn't wait to return.

When Matt got back home, we gave him an "out." He could return to a local college for second semester and look for new, broader horizons from a more familiar setting. Even though Matt appreciated our offer, he chose otherwise, determined to eke out a positive experience. So, despite our misgivings, Matt returned to CU the following term with two missions—to enjoy his time there and look for an alternate school for his sophomore year.

Though not easy by any means, Matt did manage to look more forward than back when he returned to Boulder and, following a quiet summer of reflection and reunion with high school buddies, Matt embarked on yet another adventure: moving to Boston to attend Emerson College. Emerson was as different from CU as any two places could be. It had no campus to speak of (the city was its campus), only a handful of majors to study, and class sizes that allowed everyone to know everyone else by the end of the first week. The orientation for transfer students like Matt was a whale-watching trip in the open Atlantic.

Within a week of arrival in Boston, the following arrived to our Ohio home:

September 9

Dear Mom and Dad:

It is my belief that with each passing moment in time, there is one individual who basks in a spotlight given only for himself: one person echoing the famous words of Lou Gehrig. Somehow, though, somehow the many moments of my past week in Boston have not seen a change in the spotlight—it's been me repeating, as Lou Gehrig said, that I am the luckiest man in the world.

Tomorrow's greeting of day brings with it the beginning of a new school year, a time of change, hope and wonder. As this evening's darkness beckons me to slumber, I rest knowing that there is no other place for me to be as happy, as optimistic, and as at ease as that of my current state, and the 'morrow's morning brings not solely a ray of sunshine for all to see, but a spotlight for me to walk in once again.

I truly thank each of you for all you have given me—friendship, love, care and opportunity—for these are the happiest days of my life. Thank you for sharing them with me.

My love and sincerity,
Matt

As parents, it was much easier to get a letter like this from Emerson than it was to receive the one from CU. During the time of this emotional upheaval with Matt, we were frequently at wit's end as to how to help, just as he was at wit's end in trying to articulate the source of his discomfort. In the 20/20 vision that accompanies retrospection, though, we did establish some things we did right, even if by chance:

- We listened to Matt and, instead of trying to take away his grief and disillusionment or dismiss them as simply growing pains or trying to get comfortable in an unfamiliar setting, we let him know that he could call us whenever he needed to. Even if all he had to talk about was his continued confusion, a voice from home provided comfort.
- We didn't try to come to fast, artificial solutions, nor did we try to erase his anxieties by telling him to just keep so busy that he didn't have time to think about how sad he was.
- We reminded Matt that since he was little, he had had big thoughts to share and people with whom to share them. We gave him a task to find one adult at CU who could serve as that sounding board; a comforting, nonjudgmental listener. He found such a person in one of his course instructors who graciously took Matt under her wing. When he told us her name, we asked if we could call her. Matt said yes, and the lines of communication between us and his newfound confidant seemed to erase many of those 1,200 miles. To this day,

we acknowledge this wonderful woman's efforts on Matt's behalf.

- We let Matt be in charge of finding his own resolution to the issue of what to do, and where to go, after CU, offering to help whenever he asked us to do so. This gave him a sense of both power and purpose, as his actions were directed to problem solving, rather than simply how sad he felt.

- When Matt decided on a new choice for college, we asked only enough questions to express our interests. Our son had given much thought to the next stage of his growth, and the last thing he needed from us was a lot of questions that doubted the logic of his choices.

- Just like when Matt played soccer in elementary school, we stood on the sidelines, cheering his triumphs and consoling him during his defeats. He took center stage to his future; we were merely his roadies.

Years later, with Matt now out of college and enjoying his life and career in his chosen field, we took time to talk about his Colorado experiences. Time had blurred (for him, not us) the dire straits he was in at the time, and as we recounted our own fears and anxieties, he was surprised by their intensity. "I didn't know," he told us, "I just saw you as being there and being strong for me." Such is a parent's role, I guess: to be a calm port in a sea of testy waters.

The biggest lesson I took away from this incident is that when you write out your dreams, do so in pencil. If the dreams stay true and focused, you can still read them in the rich, dark script in which they were written. However, if you need to change your dreams, or alter them entirely, it is much easier to erase pencil than pen, allowing you to move on to a different dream with a clean, unencumbered slate.

Goal Setting That Matters

Imagine going to the best buffet in Las Vegas, where food overflows in ridiculous excess, and being told upon entry that although there are more than 300 selections to choose from, you are welcome to taste only one item. "Take as much as you want of this single dish," says the maître d'hotel, "but make sure to limit your choice to that one favorite food."

Talk about an unappetizing situation, huh?

I often find that gifted children and teens (especially teens) find these same difficult choices, as they maneuver through school and life, wondering which one of life's buffet selections they should opt to taste. What sports or musical instruments should they play, when each provides its own kind of release and fun? What books should they read among the many thousands that sound appealing enough to devour in a night? What career should they pursue when forensic science sounds as intriguing as archaeology, as both involve digging around to find the truth? So many choices, so little time!

In addition to the difficulty of selecting "one special thing" that will make your life enjoyable and personally satisfying, there is a related dilemma—figuring out whether the goals you have set to achieve are actually your goals at all. Let me explain.

Gifted children are often better at attaining goals than they are at setting them. Being smart kids, many are able to accomplish tasks with little or no struggle. But what is the source of this success? Did these able young people set out to pave their own paths, or did they merely take a stroll down a road whose destination was set by others? Straight A's are earned in courses that high school counselors chose for you. Varsity letters are awarded for accomplishments in areas where teachers or coaches encouraged your competition "because you are one of my strongest team members." Spelling bee ribbons are hung around the necks of winning fourth graders who succeeded, in part, because Cousin Sally drilled them with words every time she babysat. In other words, gifted children are often successful in achieving goals that have been laid out for them by others. Remember that distinction between risk-taking and risk-making? This is what it looks like up close.

Gifted children are often better at attaining goals than they are at setting them.

But really, is there anything wrong with directing our kids' choices toward some things we think they'd enjoy? If done to excess, my answer is yes. The problem is that some gifted children—and by no means, *all* of them—have difficulty making their own independent decisions about what life goals to pursue because someone else in charge has always made these choices for them. At times, this external nudge to pursue a goal is quite subtle, as in the teacher who sends home a note about how "wonderful" it will be if 9-year-old Julia would become the youngest student ever to take part in the school's Geography Bee, or the grandmother who cajoles Joey into playing the clarinet because "your grandfather always wanted to do it, but he never had *your* musical talents." Subtle but effective, the pressure to attain a goal in order to bring satisfaction to someone other than yourself is a common occurrence for lots of gifted kids. The end result can be a child who is not only dependent on praise for doing well, but is also reliant on others to lay out the goals in life worth pursuing.

So the problem is two-pronged, beginning with others setting out a gifted child's goals, followed by said child's inability to determine which of life's many goals are worth "tasting," and which are best left off one's plate. Further exacerbating this dilemma is the reality of what happens when one of the goals being pursued requires intense and sustained attention if it is to be realized. Here's the truth: Few musicians become virtuosos by practicing here and there, whenever they get the urge. And few surgeons perfect their craft by scheduling their hospital rotations around their bowling league schedules. No, in order to excel, three things are needed: practice, practice, and practice.

It's time, then, to sit down with your gifted child or adolescent and look at the specifics of effective goal setting, with a few twists that they don't often hear. Twists like these:

- *You can be good at something you don't enjoy doing.* So often, gifted children and teens are competent in many areas. So, it is natural to assume that a student with a 100% grade average after 10 years of math classes actually *likes* math—yet, that is just an assumption. Your math-whiz kid may just be adept at a skill that is not really enjoyed. Too, a student who can skate around the ice and score goals with ease may like hockey but not love it. Just because a person excels in an activity or subject does not imply that he wants to pursue it with intensity, but to the teachers or coaches who observe this excellence from nearby, it is a logical leap to assume that excellence brings ardor. It doesn't always, and it doesn't have to. Your support of their *nonsupport* of something they are good at but no longer wish to pursue gives them license to move forward, unapologetically, to other ventures.

- *Anything worth doing . . . is worth doing poorly.* Gifted individuals grow so accustomed to doing many tasks without breaking an actual or intellectual sweat that the first setback, even a small one, can cause them to abandon a goal. For the gifted person who lives by the common (but erroneous) maxim that "anything worth doing is worth doing well," it is often believed that *doing well* arrives on one's first attempt. If it doesn't, then look elsewhere for satisfaction. However, if you can pursue a new area of interest with the idea that you are going to mess up, blow it big-time, look like a fool, embarrass yourself as never before, or look stupid instead of smart, then you will no doubt have what it takes to win! "Anything worth doing is worth doing poorly" is a great attitude for attempting new endeavors, for there are often only two things that separate *poorly* from *well*: time and practice. Imagine this: If you love music and always wanted to play the guitar, would you put that Fender CN-60S down on first try if you couldn't master a Bob Dylan-like fret sequence? Probably not. Instead, you'd realize that "getting to good" takes more than one attempt. Even if you're not a musician, your kids need to hear how this guitar example resonates with your own life of triumphs and defeats.

- *Some of the most worthwhile goals will be neither fully attained nor measurable.* If your goal is to become a better friend, how do you know when you get there? If your ambition is to make a positive difference in the world daily, will you stop trying to do so once your good deed for the day is done? If becoming rich and famous is important to you, when will you know you are rich, and will this richness be measured solely in dollars? Same with fame—are you talking the cover of *People* magazine famous, or famous in the eyes of a child for whom you are a personal hero? Not all goals are readily measurable, and the standards for success may differ as one gets closer to attaining one's goal. This is neither intrinsically good nor bad; it depends on the goal and the goal setter. As I cited in an earlier chapter, quoting Annemarie Roeper (1995), some of the most memorable characters in our lives are those who are "quietly gifted"—the letter writers and bus drivers who leave an indelible impression on our souls (p. 94). As Mother Teresa said, "In this life, we cannot always do great things. But we can do small things with great love." That's a mantra with which I can live. Can you allow your gifted child to do so?

- *Not every goal is worth pursuing to its conclusion, yet take pride in its partial fulfillment.* I remember thinking how great it would be to be a member of the Appalachian Mountain Club's Four Thousand Footer Club, an informal collection of individuals who hike to the summit of every one of the more than 40 mountain peaks in New England that rise more than 4,000 feet above sea level. At age 16, this goal was (excuse the pun) lofty; at age 19, it was reachable, as I was more than halfway there; at age 22, I got my first real job, and the goal seemed less important; and by age 25, I had abandoned the goal, not out of defeat, but out of deference to other goals that were loftier in other ways. Was I a failure? By one measure, yes, as I am still 10 peaks shy of the 40 I'd need to ascend to be a full-fledged member of the Four Thousand Footer Club. But today, decades removed from my initial goal as a 16-year old, I'm okay with not having achieved the heights I had hoped, for the visual sights I saw along the way to the realization of this partially fulfilled goal are etched forever into my memory and, even today, they make me realize I was a winner with every peak conquered!

As you read this list, I hope you realize that I am not talking solely about the gifted kids you are raising—I am also talking about *you*. Yes, you. Keeping these essential caveats about goal setting, success, and lack thereof in mind, it is time for you to sit down and list the specific goals you have for yourself. If you are going to help your gifted children consider their own ambitions, it's best if you have come up with a list of life goals for yourself. Here's a primer to get started:

1. *Be specific.* A goal stated loosely is a goal not attained. So, stating that you are going to "stop procrastinating" is not going to help you get there, but saying, "When I know I have a project due, I will make a calendar to segment the work into 30-minute portions," is doable.

2. *Be realistic.* If you've never golfed in your life, then making a goal to break par within one month of taking lessons might be a tad ambitious (although you do get a gold star for following the previous guideline about being specific!). Perhaps you can hope to hit par on three out of 18 holes—how's that for a start?

3. *Be reasonable.* You are more likely to attain a goal or two if you start off with a goal or two. Frequently, it is not the difficulty of goals that keep us from attaining them; it is the number of goals we have set that is unrealistic. Start small in number and build from there.

4. *Be prepared to compromise.* A goal you set in August may not be as reachable by next June, for a variety of reasons that life throws at you. But guess what: Even if losing 30 pounds may have been your goal, and you lose only 20 pounds, you are far

ahead of where you might have been had you not dieted at all. Be kind to yourself and give yourself credit for where you have succeeded, even if it isn't to the fullest extent you had hoped.

5. *Be punctual.* Some goals will be more long-term than others, and some ambitions you have may be driven more by curiosity than passion. So, if you are thinking about writing that cookbook that you *know* is inside you, give yourself a timeline for when the chapter on "Decadent Desserts" will be written. If it's not written by your deadline, check out the reason—lack of time, lack of interest, or lack of ideas? Be honest with yourself here, and either revise or relinquish this unmet goal.

6. *Be generous.* One of the worst self-sabotaging things people do is to keep their goals to themselves, as they are afraid to share with others what it is they hope to accomplish. Why so? Because gifted adults do not want to disappoint themselves or others by stating their hopes and dreams openly and then falling short in attaining them. But here's why you *have* to share your goals with others: First, the individuals with whom you share your dreams might help you to determine if they are too numerous or ambitious. Or, these people may serve as a great source of support as you make the kind of small progress on your path to success that can be noticed more readily by alert outsiders than by yourself.

7. *Be good to yourself.* When you have reached a milestone, whether it is the loss of those first 10 pounds, or the grade of B on that killer graduate school midterm in macroeconomics, reward yourself with something sweet: a compliment to yourself, a night out, a firecracker salute in the backyard. Hey, if you don't applaud your achievements, who will?

Maybe it's human nature that people are more often ready to wallow in their defeats than to celebrate their successes. But if we do this self-badgering often enough, our kids pick up on the idea that it is more important to recognize what they *haven't done* well than what they *have done* well. You don't want to tread this path with your gifted child. Your words—but even more, your actions—will show him or her a way to live a life of exuberance.

Get a Job!

I often wonder whether being immortal would solve the problem of having to choose a life specialization, but it is a useless wish. I'm going to learn as much as I can about everything from multiverse and string theory to animal and plant form and function . . . Biophysics, oceanography, and pi are also high on my list. There is simply not enough time!
—Boy, 13, New York (Schultz & Delisle, 2013, p. 141)

Some gifted kids have two belly buttons—the natural one that comes with the territory of being human, and an artificial one that they get when well-meaning relatives point their fingers at their gut and say, "You're going to be a doctor, I just know it. You're going to be a doctor. . . . " Enough poking from enough fingers gives them that "novel navel" that is felt, if not seen.

Career selection is seldom easy, but for gifted children the choice of what to be as an adult is made more difficult due to a common affliction: *multipotentiality*. Defined loosely, multipotentiality is the ability to do many things well, due to advanced abilities, combined with an avid interest in pursuing many of these areas of strength. For decades, researchers at the University of Wisconsin studied the career paths of gifted youth (Colangelo & Zaffran, 1979). What they found, time after time, teen after teen, was that multipotentiality is both a blessing and a curse. The blessing part comes with being able to succeed at almost anything that the gifted child puts her mind toward accomplishing. The curse aspect is that no matter what career path she has envisioned, the gifted youth keeps looking backward, over her shoulder, wondering what she is missing out on due to her rabid focus on her chosen career path. A common result is a gifted college student who flits from major to major in search of an occupational Holy

Grail—the be-all and end-all profession that will be fulfilling financially, emotionally, and intellectually.

Although multipotentiality is real and can be aggravating to the point of diminishing one's spirit to pursue a specific career focus, gifted teens who suffer through it seldom get much sympathy at home or in school. Why not? Other adults who charted their own courses early on and are satisfied with their life choices see only the upside of multipotentiality. They may make silly statements like, "Gee, I wish I had *your* problem—being so smart that you have your pick of any career!" What these adults do not understand is that many gifted young adults want their careers to provide all-encompassing fulfillment. A good salary isn't sufficient to attain happiness; it merely ensures that the rut in which you find yourself can be lined with gold. In the same way, arising day after day to pursue a path that provides shallow satisfaction is not a gifted individual's vision of success. Despite comfortable outside trappings, the internal desire to become something more, something different, and something else is as annoying and constant as a poison ivy itch.

Arising day after day to pursue a path that provides shallow satisfaction is not a gifted individual's vision of success. . . . The internal desire to become something more, something different, and something else is as annoying and constant as a poison ivy itch.

There are ways parents can help their gifted children deal constructively with multipotentiality. The first thing to do is to introduce your children to the concept from an early age. For example, if they become entranced with model airplane construction at age 7, followed quickly by equally avid love affairs with botany, French cooking, and architecture, congratulate your kids on being so diverse in their interests. Encourage them to explore each pursuit until they have filled themselves with enough facts and insights to satisfy their curiosity. Remind them that the world has so many things to learn, places to see, and people to meet that it may sometimes be frustrating to not have time to explore everything and everyone that catches and sustains their interest.

Next, have your gifted children record their observations of the world around them. As a special gift for no occasion at all, buy your son or daughter a classy blank book that becomes his or her journal. Whether bound in leather or shiny, satin ribbons, the journal becomes your child's personal repository for memories of passions pursued and dreams unfurled. Ask your child to date each entry, and invite him or her to reread each section several months after writing it. As time passes, themes will likely occur, and your child's inclinations toward the arts or sciences may become more pronounced. When, years after the journal began, your kids puzzle over which of thousands of careers fits them best, their journal may provide direction. After all, if a child's first mention of becoming a writer appeared at age 8, and it reemerges again and again over the years, these innocent comments from a bygone era may be pointing your child toward the inevitable direction of becoming a wordsmith.

Another vital way to deal directly with multipotentiality is to introduce your children to people who are engaged professionally in careers that hold their interest. When your child is a preteen, this may be nothing more than a couple of hours of shadowing the veterinarian to whom you bring Fido for his annual ringworm suppository, or accompanying Uncle Ralph on his big rig to deliver Popsicles to nearby Safeway grocery stores. As your kids get a little older, the time spent can be more frequent, organized, and focused, such as a Saturday morning volunteer experience in a hospital, hospice, bakery, or library. And, as the end of high school approaches, see if there is a way for your child to earn academic credit for doing an internship during the school year or in the summer as a way to determine what fits and what doesn't in terms of career possibilities.

As a result of these experiences, the best thing you can hope for, as a parent, is not *selection* of a career, but rather *direction* toward several career options. I have long lectured, often to deaf ears, on the benefit of entering college with no major at all, keeping one's options entirely open until the gifted young adult gets exposed to the array of opportunities any institution of higher learning offers. Because the vast majority of college freshmen change their major multiple times before finally landing on the one that appears on their diplomas, my advice on this topic should be heeded, not ignored. Many gifted college students begin their freshman year convinced of the surety of their career direction, only to take an elective course in comparative religions or cultural geography and find their eyes opened, horizons broadened . . . and confusion rampant. And sadly, many of these now-confused freshmen begin to think there is something wrong with them because they can't focus on that "one thing" that they are meant to become. Guess what: *There is nothing wrong with them!* Their exposure to new ideas and intriguing topics has beguiled them since kindergarten, so why should things be any different now? If their best-laid plans of becoming a dermatologist get derailed after reading Jack Kerouac or painting their first still life with acrylics, congratulate them for being so open to new possibilities. If they flit from major to major, excited anew each time they declare another one, hold off your eye-rolls and your disillusionment with their lack of decision-making skills because, in fact, they *are* making decisions, just on a schedule that makes you feel uncomfortable.

So, should your now-grown child *still* be unable to answer that timeworn question, "What do you want to be when you grow up?", at the age of 22, congratulate him or her for leaving all options open, all possibilities within reach. At that age, and younger, it is too much to ask for surety about what he or she hopes to be doing at age 45. Your patience with their uncertainty will be much more appreciated than your impatience with their shifting career foci.

And If They Don't Want to Go to College?

I can hear your defeated tone already: "I've failed as a parent!" *All* gifted kids are supposed to go to college, right? Isn't that their collective destiny? Their path to success, fame, and financial independence?

Well . . . no. As someone who has spent his life working with gifted young adults from middle school through college age, I have found that the best candidates for entering university life directly after high school are the on-beam high achievers who have always lived by the dictum of "*When* I go to college," not "*If* I go to college." These young people are prepared, academically and emotionally, for a path that they have trod well in the past—classes, exams, books, and deadlines. Other than the usual pangs of homesickness and the occasional feeling of being overwhelmed by their workloads, these students navigate the college waters successfully. They are enrolled in higher education because it is their choice to be there; they don't need parents or older siblings to tell them the importance of a college degree, because they are convinced personally that college is exactly where they belong at this point in their lives. Kudos to these individuals! They know their strengths, and they pursue them with full force.

Then there are the other kids, the ones who either do not go to college directly from high school or who do so only under duress. Whether these gifted students found success in high school or slid by with a GPA just high enough to graduate, they saw that first June morning of not having to get up for a 7:45 a.m. American Government class as a release from the binds that had tied them up for 13 years. The idea of returning to that same rigid schedule for 4 additional years of more-of-the-same is as painful to them as a tooth extraction without Novocain.

So, what do you do if you happen to be the parent of a gifted teenager who is not interested in the college route? First, realize that you need to hear your son's or daughter's reasons for wishing to bypass this experience. Perhaps the career your child is interested in pursuing is one that does not require a typical undergraduate degree. If it is more vocational, technical, or artistic in focus, a liberal arts college or research-focused university might be a bad fit from the get-go. In this case, explore options that are targeted toward the specific skill development needed to become a welder, a painter, or a website developer. Or, perhaps, like countless other high school graduates, your college-averse teens have no clue what the future holds for them, but they don't think they'll find it on a campus littered with other 18-year-olds who are equally as confused about their futures. Or maybe they are simply tired, and would like a year to do something other than study, like test their emerging adult wings in the world of work or community service. Some might choose military service, a multiyear commitment that is as legitimate an option as attending a 4-year college. Whatever their choices . . . whatever their reasons . . . the best thing you can do is acknowledge that now, as the adults they are, the decision is theirs to make. Coax, cajole, or threaten at your own risk, as these disrespectful responses will likely be ignored by the gifted young adult seeking answers that may take longer than the timeline you've established in your mind, as the parent.

The best thing you can do with your college-averse kid is to ask for some ideas of options that she has been considering. Because it is often easier to figure out what you *don't* want instead of what you *do* want, this may take some time and effort on your teen's part. Call in any reinforcements you have—guidance counselors, personal counselors, trusted friends, teens who have taken paths that did not include college, or others whom your child is willing to listen to and learn from.

Next, if and when your gifted teen chooses a direction to pursue, be as excited about this college alternative as he is. The greatest alliances with our children are forged when we show genuine interest in something that is important to them. Maybe working full time at Old Navy while taking fashion design courses at a nearby center for the arts is not your idea of a year well spent. But, if this is your child's plan, and he has articulated well why this is important to him, your support will show a level of trust that will be appreciated greatly.

Will your gifted son or daughter *ever* attend college? Much will depend on how his or her goals play out during this first year of independence from high school. If she sees the need for specific courses that only higher education can provide, or if a trusted mentor with whom she worked has convinced her of the benefit of such a choice, then higher education may, indeed, be in the picture. *This* time, though, your young adult offspring will be going out of personal volition, not a parental nudge. In the long run, this one year (or longer) of personal exploration may be exactly what is needed to focus a bright adolescent toward a career path that is both personally and fiscally sustaining.

Olivia Fauland, a gifted young woman who took a "gap year" (the popular term for deferring college), chose to do a cultural exchange in Sweden through American Field Services (AFS). Living with a Swedish family, not speaking the language, and finding even basic tasks like grocery shopping overwhelming, Olivia confessed that the first few weeks abroad were some of the hardest times in her life. But, upon reflection at her year's end, Olivia wrote this:

> I realized that I am capable of anything and have the ability to adapt to my surroundings without losing who I am. I learned to calm down and not be so hard on myself for making mistakes. . . . I assumed the responsibility of fending for myself and making informed decisions and judgments as an adult. My social and communication skills were taken to another level through the language barrier, allowing me to connect with people from diverse backgrounds and upbringings. . . . I have to warn that a gap year is not simply a year off, but a year of discovery and growth. . . . the benefits of taking a year to grow, mature, and learn in a different setting than a classroom is one of the best decisions I have made for my personal life, my education and my future. (Galbraith and Delisle, 2011, pp. 184–186)

As Olivia's comments about her gap year show, gifted adolescents' minds are as active and excited as when they were 6 years old. Learning continues to be a part of their everyday experiences, whether enrolled in college, teaching snowboarding in Vail, feeding downtrodden families at the local rescue mission, or mastering the art of international friendship in Sweden. For sure, it is seldom easy for a parent of a gifted kid with unlimited possibilities to accept a path after high school that doesn't follow the typical college route. So, if your gifted teen chooses an option other than college, remember these three essential P's of parenting teenagers:

- *Patience.* Not every gifted teenager's journey will end up at the same place at the same time. Eighteen is still young enough to take risks, make mistakes, and start over with a fresh set of goals. As I'll review later in Chapter 10, life is not a race to see who can get to the end the fastest.

- *Pride*. It takes guts for a gifted high school student to forego the obvious choice of college to embark on something exotic, quirky, or simply mundane. As much as this kink in the college plan may sting you initially, take pride in the fact that you have raised someone whose sense of independence allowed her to choose a separate course.

- *Persistence*. When the going gets tough, and your now-adult child begins to question the wisdom of his decisions, be the one person who does *not* say, "I told you so." Realize that few healthy people make choices knowing they are bad choices, and fewer still enter a new phase of life hoping to fail at it. By being persistently there to listen, persistently there to give advice when asked, and persistently there with a nonjudgmental outlook that reveals an abiding trust in your child's decision-making abilities, you are providing a kind of sustenance that will allow your relationship to grow stronger with each passing year.

Stepping Back . . . Stepping Out: A Fitting Chapter Conclusion

Fool that I am, I proposed a last-day-of-school writing lesson with a class of gifted eighth graders I had known for 2 years. They were in the mood for field day events, yearbook signings, and the tear-inducing end-of-year PowerPoint presentation that served as our send-off to the high school next door. But, troopers that they are, my students cut me just enough slack to let me intrude for 15 minutes on their last afternoon together as classmates. My assignment was simple: Think back on the past school year and answer two questions, "What gives you hope?" and "What gives you joy?"

Write your dreams in pencil . . . so when you need to change them, you can start with a clean slate all over again.

The room grew silent—there's a first time for everything with eighth graders—as I distributed paper and pencils, awaiting their responses. Here are a few of the statements my eighth graders made.

It gives me hope . . .
- when I see a friend succeed in something I helped them learn
- when I think of my parents still being alive when I am an adult
- when I dream of my college football team raising the crystal football after being declared national champs
- when a very biased person changes their mind
- when I see my mother going through so much, and still being strong and never hanging her head in shame
- when I see that only a few girls have someone to dance with
- when my mother says "see you later," instead of "goodbye"
- when I see another meal is on the table

It gives me joy . . .
- when I make babies laugh
- when girls come up behind me and put their hands over my eyes and make me guess who it is
- when I finish a good book and see the world from the eyes of a character in it
- when I read Maya Angelou's poem, "Phenomenal Woman"
- when I hear preschoolers singing their ABCs
- when my brother gives me a ride to school happily, with no complaints

- when I wake up on a summer morning, greeted by the sun, and realize that this day has the potential to be the best one of my life

As the students read their responses out loud, their individual and collective voices grew stronger and richer. When the last item was read, a palpable energy infused the room; we were excited and exhausted simultaneously, and this tribute to ourselves and those who cared about us made us realize just how much we had learned this year, not just about academics, but also about ourselves.

"Write your dreams in pencil," I advised the students, "so when you need to change them, you can start with a clean slate all over again."

I wished them well as I thought back to the time when I gave my son the same message years ago. And as they left our classroom for the final time minutes later, we shared hugs, high-fives and warm, embracing handshakes. It was time for them to move on, and with a helping hand from home, their journeys will take them down many roads that lead to some intriguing destinations.

Gifted Children Speak Out

"My future goals? To achieve. To know. To learn. To explore the full range of my abilities. To write. To express. To discover. To impart. To teach. To communicate."

—Girl, 13, England

"I have no idea what to become. Every time I consider a career, it is always shattered by the reality of the job and how much school the profession entails."

—Boy, 16, Wisconsin

"I plan on taking life as it comes at me. Trying to plan too much just sets you up for failure and high anxiety. I'm not into the whole rat race thing."

—Boy, 17, Nevada

"I want to dance in my old ballet class, play my clarinet, draw thousands of pictures (good ones), create beautiful pieces of woodwork, cook and sew for my children, decorate my home, be an astrophysicist, go to Mars, and understand all of my questions about life. That's not too much to ask, is it?

—Girl, 17, Pennsylvania

Chapter 9

Make a Life, Not Just a Living

I was flying to yet another consulting gig to give a talk about teaching and living with gifted kids. As usual, pen in hand, I scribbled comments on some of my students' assignments. First, I tackled a few projects completed by my college undergraduates; later, I moved on to my eighth graders' essays about the historical figure whom they most resembled in terms of motives and goals.

Seated beside me, expense spreadsheets in hand, was a gentleman a bit grayer than I, yet still my junior in years. As he tabulated and erased, tabulated and erased, a whirl of stale air exited his tired mouth. He seemed frustrated and as unhappy computing his calculations as I was overjoyed by evaluating my students' prose.

Reacting without thinking, I pulled out a couple of pages of my eighth-grade students' writing. I chose Gwen's reflection on the life of Amelia Earhart and how Gwen wished to someday have Amelia's spirit of adventure, as well as Tommy's essay on Dr. Richard Olney, a man who studied the causes of Lou Gehrig's disease for 25 years before, ironically, contracting and dying from the disease he was trying to cure. To Gwen and Tommy, these two people were personal heroes with whom they felt a close connection. Breaking my vow to never talk to the person sitting beside me on a flight, I turned to this jetlagged stranger and asked a simple question:

"Would you like to read what my eighth graders wrote about someone they admire?"

Patrick—that was his name—looked perplexed at this intrusion of the personal space barrier we had both erected. Caught off guard, he gave only a polite, "Uh . . . sure," as he took the papers from my outstretched hand. He read them with an intensity I had not noted when he was examining his expense spreadsheets.

"Got any more of these?" Patrick asked after several minutes.

"Just about 80 of them," I replied.

Patrick smiled, took a quick gulp of his drink, and said something that reinforced what I already knew: "You're a lucky man."

For the remainder of the flight, Patrick and I read essay after essay. He'd often pick out a line or two that made him think or laugh, and show it to me as a proud parent might display the newest photo of his twins. Eventually, I invited him to make any comments he would like on the papers, telling him that 13-year-olds would enjoy hearing from someone other than their teacher about the power of their words.

As landing neared, he read faster, hoping to get as many papers completed as he could. His comments were rich with warranted praise and poignant assessments of the depth of spirit most students' essays displayed. Upon disembarking, I thanked Patrick for the help; he thanked me for the chance to do, in his words, "finally . . . something important."

It was obvious Patrick enjoyed the material trappings of success—an expensive suit, a designer wristwatch, and a first-class plane ticket—but such luxuries, once attained, returned as little satisfaction as did completing his expense reports. Reading eighth graders' personal essays, though . . . now *there* was something that made a man rich.

To live a life of hollow achievement dries up even the most ardent of spirits.

Some of you might be asking what this diversion has to do with this book's content and message, but my guess is that most of you already catch my drift—to live a life of hollow achievements dries up even the most ardent of spirits. So, picking up where the last chapter left off, Chapter 9 is going to focus on the importance of making a difference in the lives of others.

The Importance of Importance

When you are 13 years old and you have an entire page of *Entrepreneur Magazine* devoted to you (Juergen, 2011), you must have done something unexpected. Hart Main did just that. Here's Hart's story. His younger sister was selling candles for a school fundraiser. Hart, sniffing the products, noticed that they smelled . . . well, "girly": like roses, strawberries, vanilla. Hart thought to himself, "No dude will ever buy these candles."

So, using $100 of his savings from his paper route, plus a $200 loan from his parents, Hart decided to begin making candles that guys' noses would appreciate. His initial candle scents included freshly cut grass, new baseball mitt, bacon, sawdust, and campfire. He made his candles in soup cans, naming his Company "ManCans," and marketed them by going door-to-door to area merchants in his hometown of Marysville, OH, asking them to take his candles on consignment.

That was in 2011, and today, ManCans is not only doing well, but it has also expanded way beyond Marysville. With sales of more than 300,000 candles thus far (including new scents of Memphis barbeque, flapjacks, and more), Hart has lived up to the hype that brought him to the pages of *Entrepreneur Magazine* in the first place. He recently sold his candle company to a nonprofit business, Beaver Creek Candle Company; he and his dad wrote a book about their experiences, *One Candle, One Meal*; and Hart is now majoring in economics and criminal justice at the university where I worked for 25 years, Kent State University in Ohio.

Oh yeah, and that "One Meal" aspect of his book's title? You see, not only is Hart a successful businessman, he is a generous one. For, with each candle he sells, Hart donates a meal to one of 25 homeless shelters located in four different states. That's a lot of meals for a lot of hungry people.

What caused Hart to take a rather simple idea—making candles in scents that guys liked—and take it to a place that benefits humanity? Hart is not alone in his desire to improve the world through individual support of good causes—countless kids do so every day, in big and small ways. Still, not every kid sees as vividly as does Hart just what an impact a person can make on others by simply stretching himself into new directions. In *The Merchant of Venice*, William Shakespeare wrote, "How far a little candle throws its beams. So shines a good deed in a weary world." Let's see what you can do, as a mom or dad, if you happen to live with one of those kids for whom philanthropy and empathy are simply a part of their DNA, and whose candle beams shine so brightly.

Teaching Gifted Kids to Care: Character Development in Action

Thomas Lickona (2004), a champion of the character education movement, noted that our two goals as parents are to help our children become smart and to help them become good. Gifted kids, by virtue of intellects that rise higher and faster than those of their age-mates, have the *smart* part down pat. The *good* part may not come as naturally, yet the opportunities are often there to expose our children to actions that they can take to help the world in big or small ways.

It is often remarked that gifted children are more aware of the world around them and the pain and anguish it often contains. They read news online and cringe at the thought that countless acres of rainforest are being destroyed in the name of economic development, or their hearts break as they learn of a local family who has lost all they owned in a fire, including both pets and possessions. Or they hear of yet another school shooting and not only worry about if their school will be next, but also about the lives of the surviving parents whose children have been murdered in Newtown or Parkland or Santa Fe. When they see instances of the world going awry, gifted kids often feel helpless to do anything to make a change, as they know in some uncanny way that change is long, difficult, and complicated.

When confronted with the realities of a world that is not always kind nor fair, gifted kids react with the same variety of responses that the rest of us do—some get angry, some get sad, some ignore their feelings, and some choose to make a difference. If your child falls into this last group and is determined to patch even a small hole in life's fabric, you will be put in the uneasy position of having to help your child decide how to proceed. Why uneasy? Well, unless you are a social activist yourself, you might find yourself unsure of what advice to give—who to talk to, how much to say, and what to do if your child's help is ignored. Much like a coach, you will need to stay on the sidelines as your son or daughter progresses down a path that can be pitted with disappointments, as the adults your child is trying to help or whose opinions he or she is trying to sway look at your 10-year-old as "just a kid," a young someone without power, still 8 years away from being able to vote. You want your child to succeed, of course, but you don't want to be so obtrusive as to take over his mission and make it your own. What to do?

Follow Hart Main's parents' lead: Provide emotional support and a $200 loan (if you can) so that your gifted, caring child can act upon the very real and visceral reactions he or she has to life's inequities. This may lead your child and you down paths you never anticipated following, and even if some lead to dead ends, your child will know that you are in his corner when it comes to trying to make the world a little better, a little kinder, or a little more generous than it is today.

Where to Begin

If you are looking for ways to help your child become more aware of the meaningfulness of even the smallest of kind acts done genuinely, you need search no further than the local newspaper. As both a teacher and a dad, I have done this often. In school, in fact, I began a program for fourth through sixth graders entitled "Project Person to Person," in which it became the task of a group of these bighearted volunteers to scour our local newspaper, *The Plain Dealer*, and find people in our community who needed one of two things—help or a thank-you. Here are some of the people we contacted:

- Brian, a man who had suffered a stroke at age 29, recovered partially from it, and then had a second stroke when someone threw a rock through his car window, striking him in the head. Our students wrote cards and sent letters filled with hopeful wishes for a full recovery, followed 2 months later with a video that included bad karaoke renditions of our favorite winter holiday songs. Eventually, Brian contacted us with his own song—the most effective way he could communicate was by singing—and his wife and two young children visited our classroom several times, cementing a multiyear bond of hope between strangers.

- Matt is the oldest of four children whose mom and dad were both killed in separate accidents, a year apart. News reports stated that Matt, a college junior with dreams of becoming a teacher, would have to drop out of college to get a job to support his three younger sisters. In a schoolwide project called "Links for Life," our students created and sold "chains" made from recycled paper for 10 cents each, with the goal of "uniting" our school by encircling it with the paper links that were purchased by grandparents, neighbors, and others who heard of our project. At an all-grades assembly 2 weeks later, Matt came to address our student body of 800, and to collect a check for more than $1,900.

- A high school in Nepal, where the library had been washed away in a typhoon, was in need of money to replace books that had been lost to the storm. Keeping in line with the theme of books, students collected their own used books and had a community sale at our school, raising more than $650 that was sent, via a local Peace Corps volunteer, to this Nepalese school.

The letters and photographs we received from the principal and students were heartwarming, and the message that the custodian had to sleep in the library so that no one would "borrow" these newly purchased and treasured books during the off hours caused our students to see the true impact and importance of their actions.

- U.S. soldiers fighting a desert war on foreign soil needed a touch of home, we thought, in their tents and barracks. So, students created muslin banners, hand decorated with wishes of good hope and thanks, and big enough to double as a sheet, if needed. The photos and e-mails returned to us from thousands of miles away gave proof to the students that, indeed, connecting with people back home, even kids you've never met, is always appreciated by our faraway soldiers.

One need only interview several of the children whose actions made a direct impact on the lives of another to see that the true measure of learning has little to do with texts and lots to do with *context*—learning as it occurs in the real world.

Sadly, in today's school climate of raising student test scores at all costs, there will be those who criticize such projects as being superfluous to the learning process. But one need only interview several of the children whose actions made a direct impact on the lives of another to see that the true measure of learning has little to do with texts and lots to do with *context*—learning as it occurs in the real world. You see, in order to appropriately respond to Brian, who suffered two strokes, students first had to learn what a stroke is and what its aftereffects are likely to be. (Too, they had to hone their letter-writing skills.)

In order to encircle our school with paper links, students had to determine the diameter of a link, the perimeter of the school, and how many links it would take to complete our task. (Looks a lot like math to me!)

Our students' idea of a library was a permanent structure with multiple rooms, rows and rows of books, and air-conditioned comfort. They learned that in Nepal, the library was a temporary building constructed out of any available materials, housing several hundred books, at most. (Our fifth graders had to locate Nepal; learn of its cultures, history, topography, and climate; and understand what a typhoon really is.)

Many a student had a dad, brother, mom, or cousin who was stationed overseas for a year or more, fighting in a war that is very controversial. Still, "Support Our Troops" became the rallying cry, even if some students questioned the actions that sent us there initially. (A sixth grader's observation—"So, what gives in the Middle East and Afghanistan? It seems like there have always been wars there."—posed in innocence and with curiosity, led to much historical analysis of these volatile regions of our world.)

You catch my drift, I'm sure: Character education, if done correctly, teaches gifted children much about this world that they are enmeshed in trying to decipher. Basic skills? There seems to me no more basic a skill than gaining some insights into the beauty and frailty of the human condition. And if kids happen to pick up some math or geography skills along the way, so much the better.

As a parent, there is no need for you to wait until schools come around once again to recognizing the importance of programs like "Project Person to Person" (which was eliminated, by the way, once I moved on to a different school district, as the curriculum coordinator did not believe that such activities addressed the particular academic standards our school district was trying to attain). If, however, you are lucky enough to have a supportive school administration that sees the ultimate benefit in projects like these, then work with the staff gleefully in advancing student learning that encompasses the world beyond the classroom confines. If you don't have such school district support, never fear. Instead, find ways that you, as a family, can contribute to our world in ways that make your gifted children feel as if they have something to offer back to people they know, or even those that they shall never meet. As I recommended earlier, the local newspaper is a good place to begin, but if your child is involved with organized activities—Boy or Girl Scouts, for example—or you have taken up a hammer for Habitat for Humanity, you already have access to multiple ways of helping.

One of the leading programs for helping gifted kids take hold of their futures by instituting projects that have both local and global positive ramifications is the Young Scholars Ambassador Program (YSAP) administered by the Davidson Institute for Talent Development (https://www.davidsongifted.org). More than a decade in formation, the YSAP was designed to foster learning and civic engagement through community service, volunteerism, and leadership in middle and high school students. The YSAP has resulted in dozens of student-designed projects that make our world more whole. Among the 2019 YSAP participants are these (Davidson Institute for Talent Development, n.d.):

- Dimitri, age 14, who designed a scientific, comprehensive, and accessible anti-drug education campaign focusing on both street and prescription drugs, and their abuses.
- Dana, age 13, who developed "A Chance to Dance," a program that offers ballroom dancing to middle and high school students who are wheelchair-bound.
- Rex, age 16, who developed a program in which teens read to elderly residents of nursing homes and retirement centers, connecting generations in important and loving ways.
- Tanya, age 13, whose project, "Motion for the Ocean," brings awareness to kids on the impact of man-made debris on the health of marine life.

As stated so well by that gifted grandmother of mine, Annemarie Roeper (1995),

Children need to live in a world that is relevant. They need to grow in an educational environment that prepares them to make sense of the real world and gives them the tools to change it. The difference is that gifted children know this and can articulate it, while others just accept it. (p. 142)

Who among us has not met a 12-year-old who is "gifted in the heart," preternaturally aware of the scope of the issues that everyday people face every day? Who among us has not seen a gifted teenager angry at some arbitrary decision that reduces another individual's dignity or autonomy? Who among us has not comforted a gifted young person who saw vividly the dissonance between an adult's words and his or her actions? For the greatest reason of all—the preservation of hope—character education is as basic a skill as you can imagine. Indeed, in today's complex world, learning to care is as important as learning to read.

"Being" Versus "Doing"

So much of what I detail in this chapter highlights the merits of gifted children's and teens' actions on behalf of others. These are beautiful, selfless acts that deserve our attention, and I applaud any young person who endeavors to increase the world's quotient of beauty, tolerance, or kindness.

However, there are probably some of you reading this who do not see your child as being this self-starter, this enlightened entrepreneur with a fully developed social conscience. Does that imply your kid is a "moral slacker," a selfish ingrate whose favorite word is *me*? That is certainly not my intent, to compare gifted children on a scale of goodness—and it should not be your intent, either.

Here's why: Like the rest of us, gifted children come in all shapes and sizes when it comes to individual personality attributes. Some, like the Davidson Young Ambassadors that I mentioned previously, are very vocal and public about their ambitions to improve the world through one act of kindness at a time. Other gifted children, though, are more likely to while away the hours in search of self-understanding or personal enjoyment without much outward interest in making the world a better place. If you have one of these children, enjoy him for the qualities that best define him: fun, introspection, a quiet passion for learning, or a rabid interest in lacrosse.

There's a reason that you should not try to mold your gifted child into something she is not. Here it is: Too often in our culture, gifted children have been regarded as our next generation's movers and shakers who will transform our world from malignant to benign. But, if I hear one more time that the reason we need gifted programs is because "these kids will be tomorrow's leaders," I think I'll toss my cookies. The proper rationale for offering appropriate school services to gifted children is because *today* they have learning needs that are not addressed in grade-level curriculum, and just as with any other child with a special learning need, these services should be delivered *today*. We should never predicate children's current educational needs on some distant future benefit that they might afford us. None of us know what the future holds for ourselves or our kids, but we do have *today* to try to make a positive difference in their educations, both inside of school and outside of it.

Who knows? One day, not too long from now, a gifted kid may grow up to cure cancer—but then again, this cure might come from a team of talented scientists, some of whom we never classified as gifted. Or, the next great president, able to bridge the yawning and growing gap evident in our nation's politically and culturally divided populace, may be someone whose social savvy and profound knowledge of history are as galvanizing as they are rare. Identified as gifted as a child? Who would care?

Doing gifted things and *being gifted* may or may not overlap. And although we acknowledge the "doers" because their talents are displayed so evidently or obviously, let us not do so at the expense of the gifted "beings" whose insights into self and others might be heightened to the point where, very quietly, they make differences in the lives of others by being a superb parent, a remarkable teacher, or a poet whose unpublished pieces are enclosed in greeting cards to friends in need of a boost.

Let us not confuse eminence with giftedness, for when we do, we eliminate as gifted those whose talents are more quiet and subtle than most. We eliminate a best friend who always has the right thing to say during the worst of times, and we eliminate children who wish only to absorb information for its own sake, to expand their minds or enhance their spirits. When we confuse eminence with giftedness, we ignore the fact that the true essence of giftedness is the intellectual and emotional agility to transcend the obvious.

When we confuse eminence with giftedness, we ignore the fact that the true essence of giftedness is the intellectual and emotional agility to transcend the obvious.

Acknowledge when your gifted child does something that improves another's life, but also hug your gifted child who comes to you with eyes wide open and says, "Dad, I just touched a tadpole for the first time. It was awesome!" Excitement in doing and excitement in being are two aspects of giftedness that are equally important.

Gifted Grown-Ups Speak Out

"I am not one to accept what everyone feels toward a certain subject. Sometimes it really bothers me if I know no one cares what's going on in this world, or the hardships of others, or maybe I'm in trouble and need help. It really makes me mad when people can see someone's in trouble yet won't stop and help, let alone laugh at someone's mishaps."
—Michael Piechowski, 2014, p. 245

"Sometimes the people with the greatest potential often take the longest to find their path because their sensitivity is a double-edged sword—it lives at the heart of their brilliance, but it also makes them more susceptible to life's pains. Good thing we aren't being penalized for handing in our purpose late. The soul doesn't know a thing about deadlines."
—Jeff Brown, 2014, p. 4

"Dear Teachers:

I am the survivor of a concentration camp. My eyes saw what no man should witness—gas chambers built by learned engineers, children poisoned by educated physicians, infants killed by trained nurses, women and babies shot and burned by high school and college students. So I am suspicious of education.

My request is: help your students become humane. Your efforts must never produce learned monsters, skilled psychopaths, educated Eichmanns. Reading, writing, arithmetic are important only if they serve to make our children more humane."

—A school principal who survived a concentration camp (as cited in Ginott, 1972)

Chapter 10

Life Is Not a Race to See Who Can Get to the End the Fastest

I n the timeless movie *The Incredibles*, Dash, a third-grade superstar of speed, is forbidden from participating in track meets because . . . well, he is simply too fast. He'll leave the competition (and his teammates) in the dust, deflating their fragile egos as they come face-to-face with their own limitations as runners.

Mr. Incredible, Dash's dad, realizes that his son is being penalized for his talents and complains loudly about America's love affair with mediocrity: It's okay for kids to be good, but not so good that it makes other kids look bad.

In the end, Dash is allowed to race, but is reminded to tone down his excess speed—after all, no need to make others look bad in front of their friends and supporters.

How often does this scenario need to take place, in various forms and contexts, before people realize that gifted children seldom have an agenda to make other people look stupid? When gifted kids perform at levels that capitalize on their strengths or talents, they are simply being who they are. To repress what they know, or what they can do, sends a clear message that excellence must be tempered with modesty. It's okay to be good, but being *too good* is bad. Real bad.

"Everyone's special, Dash," says his sister, in an attempt to mollify his disdain for not being able to display his talents fully.

"Which is another way of saying no one is," Dash responds, strongly, yet dejectedly (Walker & Bird, 2004).

In this final chapter, I will attempt to walk a fine line between defending the right to be excellent while maintaining an attitude that not everything in life must be a race to the finish line. It is often a constant battle waged between gifted kids and their parents, gifted kids and their classmates, and gifted kids and themselves, to find that elusive balance between competition and collaboration.

In Praise of Elitism

When I entered the field of gifted child education more than 40 years ago, I was like a dry sponge: I lapped up every available bead of information about gifted children, absorbing every drop of knowledge indiscriminately, noticing neither inherent conflicts in logic nor opinions that went askew to my own beliefs. But, as time progressed and my knowledge and experiences with gifted children and their advocates expanded and deepened, I began to question and challenge . . . well, everything. Like the gifted kid I once was, and the gifted adult I had grown to become, I searched my soul for the meaning and purpose behind my studies. Our field of gifted child education, although small, was filled with contradictions, as some individuals were "stingy" about defining giftedness, leaving it to those who had IQs so high that they would qualify as geniuses, while others opened the floodgates of giftedness to anyone who had an observable talent that exceeded what might be expected for a kid of a certain age. Too, some authors wrote about giftedness from the academic point of view, seeing giftedness as a school-based phenomenon, while others spoke eloquently of the emotional distinctions that permeated the hearts of gifted people.

So which was it? The stingy definition or the floodgate one? Academic achievement or emotional intensities? The questions constantly plagued me, and, at times, they still do. For example, when I define giftedness in a way that is more exclusive than inclusive (no, I do *not* believe that everyone is gifted in some capacity), I then meet a youngster who doesn't fit this mold of exclusivity, but still appears to be capable, intuitive, or sensitive beyond her years. Hmmm . . . is she gifted? And when it comes to gifted programming in schools, even though I believe it is essential that gifted kids have opportunities to get together as the intellectual and emotional peers that they are, I question if bunching them together for too much time will give them an artificial view of the world they share with nongifted others. So, where is the supposed happy medium when it comes to academic placement? And, will one gifted child's happy academic medium in school be another gifted child's academic purgatory? You'd think after more than four decades of mulling over this stuff, the answers would be clear. Not so for me.

This gnawing ambivalence I have about who is gifted and who isn't, and what to do academically with the ones who are, is counterbalanced—thankfully—with one piece of surety: I *know* that advocating for this collection of children does not make me an elitist, merely a realist. Let me try to put this issue of elitism into its proper context, as it is one that has plagued our field of study almost since its inception.

If you've been interested in gifted children's lives and educations for more than 10 minutes, you will have experienced a gifted naysayer of *The Incredibles* mindset. Believing that everyone is gifted at something, these individuals pooh-pooh the notion of giftedness as a distinct quality that some have and others do not have. If all else fails in trying to convince you of their point of view, they pull out their secret weapon from the arsenal of terms that sends shivers up the spine of anyone who lives in a democracy: *elitism*. By singling out some children as gifted, you will be told, you are downgrading the personal worth of anyone who doesn't meet your high, high standard.

. . . To which I'd respond, "horsefeathers."

Now, if by elitism you think I advocate that gifted children and adults are somehow inherently worth more than those to whom this label is not ascribed, then you have it all wrong. The brand of elitism that pegs some races or classes of people as being superior to others is absurd and offensive; such beliefs hold no place in my personal repertoire. However, if it is elitist to believe in the sanctity of human differences and to state unequivocally that an IQ of 145 *does* earmark a 10-year-old child as different from other fourth graders in some important ways, then an elitist I am. If it is elitist to take a child aside and tell her that her giftedness is a perennial quality that will allow her to experience and interpret life situations in ways that are more sophisticated and complex, then I will proudly wear the label of *elitist*. If gifted students need a foot soldier to champion their rights to express their talents fully without fear of retribution from others, or if they need someone to explain that their emotional and intellectual abilities may make them stand out from classmates in ways that require a change in curriculum or grade placement, then I will be that man.

As always, our world and our homes need the richness of spirit and compassion that gifted children provide. To abandon them to *The Incredibles* logic is to champion equity and excellence for all, making our gifted children sacrificial lambs on the altar of egalitarianism. Gifted children deserve better, and who else will take up the challenge but a bunch of elitists like you and me who realize and will be willing to accentuate an essential truth: that gifted children do exist, as they always have and always will, and to discount their presence and prominence in our world is to be the ultimate intellectual snob who would rather deny reality than face it?

When it comes to standing up for gifted individuals, am I an elitist? You bet I am . . . and proud of it.

Gifted children do exist, as they always have and always will, and to discount their presence and prominence in our world is to be the ultimate intellectual snob who would rather deny reality than face it.

On the Other Hand . . .

Similar to the law of physics that states that for every action there will be an equal and opposite reaction, the same logic applies when considering the uniqueness of each and every gifted child. For as individualistic as they are, with needs and quirks that mark them as unique even in relation to other gifted children, they also share many commonalities with other kids their age. This is the underlying reason that many gifted advocates, myself included, espouse the mantra that gifted children are children first, and gifted second. This statement in no way denigrates the importance of giftedness and its impact on many facets of the child's life. Instead, it legitimizes our common humanity.

Consider this: Not only is LeBron James an amazing basketball player, but he also started the LeBron James Family Foundation, which is dedicated to getting more than 1,000 inner-city kids into college—and making sure they graduate. And just for good measure, every night he is home, I'm sure he tucks his kids into bed. Taylor Swift is not just a worldwide singing sensation, but she was also named by *Today* as the "most charitable celebrity," thanks to her work with the Red Cross, UNICEF, the Wounded Warrior Project, and other agencies. But I bet she also calls or texts her parents regularly. Bill and Melinda Gates have transformed the world of technology, and they have also spearheaded efforts to expand access to health and education to the tune of $27 billion (. . . with a *b*). Having the financial wherewithal to do these things gives these celebrities platforms to transform their world. Yet still, Bill and Melinda go home every night to care for their kids as mom and dad.

So, if famous people can have lives beyond the roles they play in public, our gifted children need to be allowed this same courtesy. Even if your son just came in first in the countywide writing contest, or your daughter was named as a finalist for a Westinghouse scholarship, and you applaud these achievements until your hands blister . . . you should then remind your child that the dishes still need to be put away, and the toys strewn across the living room floor still need to be picked up.

This is such common sense, isn't it—treating our kids as children first, and gifted second? Yet, when you have children who are so far advanced from the intellectual or academic norm, it is too easy to put their childhoods aside and let their giftedness take prominence. Take a minute to remember that the basic needs of humans—the need to belong, the need to be accepted unconditionally by others, and the need to feel safe—are important common denominators that we all share. Yes, your child's giftedness is an important part of who he is, but it is not the *entirety* of who he is.

One gifted teenager addressed these concerns in the classic book, *On Being Gifted*, a volume in which 20 gifted teens wrote about the ups and downs of being them (American Association for Gifted Children, 1978). The following excerpt, a typical passage, addresses the desire for being recognized as the unique individual that you are, rather than the stereotypic depiction of who a gifted person is supposed to be:

> Some people are turned off by the amount of recognition I've had; some people assume I'm conceited and untouchable, or impossible to get along with. *They've heard of me but they don't know me in person; they've read the reviews and think they've read the book.* People are prone to jump to conclusions about me solely because of any "gifted" image I may have; some people have already made up their minds about me or think I could never be interested in their more mundane things like parties and girls.

> On the whole, though, I have to confess that I'd rather be a troubled "genius" and a "struggling young writer" than a straight-C student who spends free weekends carrying bags at the A & P. (p. 20)

This young man's desire to fit in is a developmentally appropriate reaction—after all, what teenager, gifted or otherwise, doesn't want to feel a sense of belonging with age-mates? Yet still, his desire to maintain the integrity of his own uniqueness also plays a prominent role in his growth toward adulthood. Maturity and life experiences will orient gifted kids like these toward a path of either unique recognition or blind conformity. The choice is theirs, not ours, but if we can help to guide our children through the sometimes uncomfortable churning waters that accompany adolescence, they may emerge from the teenage rapids as individuals who are so comfortable in their own skin that the opinions of others hold little sway over the life decisions they ultimately make.

Acknowledge [your children's] insights and global awareness of issues, and then go out and have a snowball fight, toss a Frisbee with them and the dog, build a house out of playing cards, or splash each other with mud so thick that you have to hose down outside.

Respect giftedness, yes . . . but the totality of childhood and adolescence cannot and should not be ignored or demeaned as less important.

I have just one more "on the other" issue I wish to raise before closing this chapter, and this book. It involves a concept that may sound reminiscent of "The Age of Aquarius" that The 5th Dimension sang about in the 1960s, but so be it: It's the idea of living for the moment.

As mentioned in a previous chapter, from the time gifted kids are little, those who care about them often address them in the future tense. Comments like "With your abilities, you can become anything you want to be when you grow up," or "Someone with your brain will really be able to make a difference in the world" are inspiring comments to hear, yet they are laced with potential pitfalls. Not only are the children who absorb these compliments prone to wonder if their future choices will measure up to others' expectations, but they may also question if the phase of life they are in now—childhood—is merely a means to a bigger end, a staging area for their "real lives" as adults. Thankfully, it's not. Consider this reality: We are grown-ups for about 80% of our lives. And, if you parcel out the totally dependent years of infancy and preschool, that leaves only about 12% of one's life to be a kid—to be innocent of and unencumbered by adult-size worries. Yet, with many gifted children, even that smidgen of time is violated. First, their own active minds are naturally going to seek the bigger picture and the higher truths. With large vocabularies in hand, they will seek answers to questions that even we, as adults, struggle to decipher. With each question, another piece is chipped away from their childhoods, unless we decide, as adults, to let our kids be kids.

What to do? Acknowledge their insights and global awareness of issues, and then go out and have a snowball fight, toss a Frisbee with them and the dog, build a house out of playing cards, or splash each other with mud so thick that you have to hose down outside. Because, as John Ross, valedictorian of his Ohio high school, reminded his fellow graduates several years ago:

> Like countless people have asked countless other graduates, a man asked me, "What are you going to do with the rest of your life?"
>
> But as I stood there dumbfounded, eyebrows bent, mind perplexed, I realized I had no idea. And I realized, too, that it was good not to know and good not to have any idea.
>
> It was good not to know where my money will be invested in ten years or where I will be working in five. Good not to know for whom I wanted to work, or where, or why. It was good not to know how big my house will be or what car I'll drive. Good not to know about retirement or IRAs and 401K plans . . .
>
> When you plan too much, you lose important things like watching cartoons and not caring that Wile E. Coyote comes back after every ill-timed attempt with boulders. Laughing at least 37 times every day. Loving everything and everybody because the world seems like one of those books that you save for a rainy day and a soft, high-backed chair by the window.

It was good not to know what I wanted to do, because when you're young and fresh and innocent, you can't go wrong. Someone once wrote, "When you're young, you're golden." So, wherever I go and whatever I do with the rest of my life, I'll always stay young and I'll always stay golden. (Delisle & Galbraith, 2002, p. 159)

John's view of life as a series of present-tense moments to be savored, laughed about, and enjoyed to their fullest is a refreshing reminder that even though the "best is yet to come" for our gifted children in future years, there is absolutely nothing wrong with relishing each new day with an aplomb that borders on giddiness. Can we—can our children—follow John's lead?

Closing Time

For 25 years, I was a professor of gifted child education at Kent State University, a place known infamously for its place in the history, when four students were gunned down in 1970 while protesting the war in Vietnam. But to me, this academic home was a peaceful and robust environment to be a teacher. Time may never heal all wounds, but my time at Kent State was filled with glorious interactions with students excited about teaching the next generation.

Unless they opted out of the education profession after graduation, nearly all of my former undergraduate and graduate students are teachers or school administrators today. It was a remarkable, quarter-century journey for me to learn from them, and I can only hope that I impacted their professional lives in as positive a way as they impacted mine.

Inevitably, whenever I taught the introductory course "Social and Emotional Components of Giftedness," I had a series of enlightened stragglers who stayed behind after class to volunteer an admission that, truth be told, many of them felt uncomfortable sharing. Those uncomfortable conversations went something like this:

"I'm really enjoying this course, Dr. Delisle," they'd begin.

"How so?" I'd ask.

"Well" (and this is where they often begin to squirm a bit), "when I signed up for the course, I figured I'd learn something about gifted children that I could take back and use in my classroom."

" . . . And is that happening?" I would ask with anticipation.

More squirming. "Yes, it is," (followed by an extended pause).

"But, something else is happening, too," I'd suggest.

Then, the floodgates would open. Students, often with tear-filled eyes, explained how the course content—the discussion of overexcitabilities, the work of Roeper and Hollingworth, the words of gifted children discussing their own thoughts and beliefs—had caused them to come to a conclusion that they had ignored or disregarded for years: that they, or someone close to them at home, were gifted. Often, this realization came with a mixture of joy, pain, sadness, and humility, ending in a statement that is not far from this one: "All of this time, I thought I/my spouse/my daughter was just weird."

Life is not a race to see who can get to the end the fastest. Taking each day as it comes, seeing each triumph and disappointment as simply stepping-stones to all of the tomorrows that lie ahead, is a lesson you can teach your gifted kids every morning as they awake.

This oft-repeated scenario, whether in my graduate class or elsewhere, is a cathartic moment for an adult coming to grips with his or her own giftedness, or the giftedness of a loved one who has, heretofore, been misunderstood, dismissed, or looked at oddly by others. Frequently, from that moment on, these students began opening up more in class, talking of personal experiences in school or life situations that caused head nods from many of their classmates; head nods that indicated that this student was not alone in seeing giftedness from a very personal vantage point.

Way back then, one of my graduate students, Laurel K. Chehayl, took these self-revelations to a higher plain, composing a poetic tribute to her son, and to herself, as the gifted individuals that the two of them were and are. In doing so, she related what college students, parents, and gifted children themselves have been sharing with me throughout my career—the desire to be understood and accepted as gifted individuals . . . as gifted *people*. Here is Lauren's poem:

Reflection
by Laurel K. Chehayl

I have learned . . .

I'm not the only one
who feels stupid
being smart;
there may be a reason
my boy and I are feeling people—we cry
at movies, in museums,
upon reaching the ends of books.

I have learned . . .

I've not always made the best decisions
and wish I had more strength sometimes.
But I've learned, too, that my own—
and it's OK to use the word—
giftedness
has been a gift to him, to my motherhood
as I navigate with him the pain of
being told we're not living up to our
potential,
not remembering when we learned to read,
or being the only one, at 10,
with a deep passion for all things beautiful.

I have learned . . .

I've not always been the best teacher,
but I have been the best I can
and I've learned, now, because my eyes,
opening for the first time.
see who we
are, and those
that remind me of me, or him
are the ones that are like us
The gifted—
to be acknowledged, to be celebrated,
to hold up to the light in my heart,
examined and cherished.

But most importantly
I have learned
it's OK to say the word
. . . gifted. (2004, p. 4)

As this book ends, I have to wonder how many of the adults reading it did so in an effort to find answers for how to raise their own gifted children, how to understand them fully (or, at least, better), and how to convince others that having a gifted child is not as easy as it might seem. Yet, if you are like so many of my graduate students, I would bet a tidy sum that your reading has caused you the introspection Laurel discovered as she read about topics and issues that sounded familiar at a personal level; for in learning about your gifted child, some of you may have underlined passages that referred as much to you as they do to that gifted 12-year-old you've cuddled since birth. If so, welcome to the world of self-discovery!

Life is not a race to see who can get to the end the fastest. Taking each day as it comes, seeing each triumph and disappointment as simply stepping-stones to all of the tomorrows that lie ahead, is a lesson you can teach your gifted kids every morning as they awake. A new day, a fresh perspective, another reason to shine: You have within you the power to help your gifted children appreciate themselves as the competent, caring young people you have come to cherish.

Enjoy the ride!

Gifted Children Give Thanks

"My parents have many times talked to me about my special talents. I seem to accomplish in everything I do, and they realize this. They talk to me about many things, and they encourage and love me. My parents and I have a very good relationship."

—Boy, 13, Kentucky

"I sit down with my mom and watch the news. She'll discuss things with me that I don't understand. (She explains things very well, in my opinion.)"

—Boy, 14, Connecticut

"We travel to unique destinations a lot. My dad says I need to be aware of lots of places, customs, and people in order to be successful in life. I guess my parents encourage me to try new things by always doing this themselves. Our family life is one adventure after another. I think it's great.

—Girl, 17, Nevada

And finally, one last reminder that the kids you created will need the protective comfort of your love and guidance far beyond their childhood years:

Kids and Kites
by Robert J., age 11

Kites fly but they need an anchor
Kids roam but they need a home

If a kite loses its anchor, it falls
If a child loses his home, he declines

As a kite goes higher and higher
You give it more string
As a child grows older and older
You give him more freedom
But here the similarity ends
For kites (even with the most string imaginable)
Crash sooner or later
But kids
(if they are old enough)
Adjust safely and create new homes.

References

American Association for Gifted Children. (1978). *On being gifted*. New York, NY: Walker.

Assouline, S., Colangelo, N., VanTassel-Baska, J., & Lupkowski-Shoplik, A. (Eds.). (2015). *A nation empowered: Evidence trumps the excuses that hold back America's brightest students* (Vol. 2). Iowa City: University of Iowa, The Connie Belin & Jacqueline N. Blank International Center for Gifted Education and Talent Development.

Beneventi, A. (2016). The Annemarie Roeper method of qualitative assessment: My journey. *Roeper Review, 38*, 252–257.

Brown, J. (2014). *Love it forward*. Toronto, Canada: Enrealment Press.

Chehayl, L. (2004). Reflection. *Gifted Education Communicator, 35*(4), 4.

Colangelo, N., Assouline, S. G., & Gross, M. U. M. (2004). *A nation deceived: How schools hold back America's brightest students* (Vol. 1). Iowa City: The University of Iowa, The Connie Belin & Jacqueline N. Blank International Center for Gifted Education and Talent Development.

Colangelo, N., & Zaffran, R. T. (1979). *New voices in counseling the gifted*. Dubuque, IA: Kendall-Hunt.

Conley, D. (2000). *Honky*. Berkeley: University of California Press.

Davidson Institute for Talent Development. (n.d.). *2019 ambassadors*. Retrieved from http://www.davidsongifted.org/Young-Scholars/Program-Benefits/Ambassador-Program/2019-Ambassadors

Delisle, J. R. (2005). *Once upon a mind: The stories and scholars of gifted child education*. Boston, MA: Cengage Learning.

Delisle, J. R. (2015). Differentiation doesn't work. *Education Week*. Retrieved from https://www.edweek.org/ew/articles/2015/01/07/differentiation-doesnt-work.html

Delisle, J. R. (2018). *Doing poorly on purpose: Strategies to reverse under-achievement and respect student dignity*. Alexandria, VA: ASCD.

Delisle, J., & Galbraith, J. (2002). *When gifted kids don't have all the answers: How to meet their social and emotional needs*. Minneapolis, MN: Free Spirit.

Delisle, J., & Lewis, B. A. (2003). *The survival guide for teachers of gifted kids: How to plan, manage, and evaluate programs for gifted youth K–12*. Minneapolis, MN: Free Spirit.

Delisle, J., & Schultz, R. A. (2016). The legacy of George and Annemarie Roeper. *Roeper Review, 38*, 213–215.

Douglas, D. (2018). *The power of self-advocacy for gifted learners: Teaching the four essential steps to success*. Minneapolis, MN: Free Spirit.

Ferrucci, P. (2009). *What we may be: Techniques for psychological and spiritual growth*. Los Angeles, CA: TarcherPerigree.

Fiedler, E. D. (2015). *Bright adults: Uniqueness and belonging across the lifespan*. Tucson, AZ: Great Potential Press.

Gagné, F. (2004). A differentiated model of giftedness and talent (DMGT): Year 2000-update. *High Ability Studies, 15*, 119–147.

Galbraith, J., & Delisle, J. (2011). *The gifted teen survival guide: Smart, sharp and ready for (almost) anything*. Minneapolis, MN: Free Spirit.

Gallagher, J. (1975). *Teaching the gifted child* (2nd ed.). Boston, MA: Allyn & Bacon.

Gardner, H. (1983). *Frames of mind*. New York, NY: Basic Books.

Ginott, H. (1972). *Teacher and child*. New York, NY: Avon.

Goleman, D. (1995). *Emotional intelligence.* New York, NY: Bantam.

Hollingworth, L. S. (1942). *Children above 180 IQ Stanford-Binet: Origin and development.* Yonkers-on-Hudson, NY: World Book Company.

Juergen, M. (2011). Teenager finds a niche in man-scented candles. *Entrepreneur.* Retrieved from https://www.entrepreneur.com/article/220259

Kane, M. M. (2011). *Reducing stress and anxiety in gifted children: The role of contemplative practice* [PowerPoint slides]. Retrieved from http://www.district158.org/weblinks/Gifted%20&%20Talented/Presentations/COCG%20-%20Reducing%20Stress%20and%20Anxiety%20in%20Gifted%20Children.pdf

Lamott, A. (2013). Me, the overly sensitive child. *Salon.* Retrieved from https://www.salon.com/2013/10/28/me_the_overly_sensitive_child

Lickona, T. (2004). *Character matters: How to help our children develop good judgment, integrity, and other essential virtues.* New York, NY: Touchstone.

Lombroso, C. (1893). *The man of genius.* London, England: Scott.

Maisel, I. (2013). *What it takes.* Retrieved from https://alumni.stanford.edu/get/page/magazine/article/?article_id=66225

Marks, G. (2016). These are the 8 dumbest research studies of 2016. *Entrepreneur.* Retrieved from https://www.entrepreneur.com/article/275060

Medvec, V. H., Madey, S. F., & Gilovich, T. (1995). When less is more: Counterfactual thinking and satisfaction among Olympic medalists. *Journal of Personality and Social Psychology, 69,* 603–610.

Minnesota Educators of the Gifted and Talented. (2008). *Responding to the needs of gifted boys.* Retrieved from http://www.grantsandresearchhelp.us/MegtPositionPaper-Gifted-Boys.pdf

Morelock, M. J. (1992). Giftedness: The view from within. *Understanding Our Gifted, 4*(3), 1, 11–15.

National Association for Gifted Children. (2010). *Redefining giftedness for a new century: Shifting the paradigm* [Position statement]. Retrieved from http://www.nagc.org/sites/default/files/

Position%20Statement/Redefining%20Giftedness%20for%20 a%20New%20Century.pdf

Neihart, M., Pfeiffer, S., & Cross, T. L. (2015). *The social and emotional development of gifted children: What do we know?* (2nd ed.). Waco, TX: Prufrock Press.

Piechowski, M. M. (1986). The concept of developmental potential. *Roeper Review, 8,* 190–197.

Piechowski, M. M. (1991). Emotional development and emotional giftedness. In N. Colangelo & G. A. Davis (Eds.), *Handbook of gifted education* (pp. 285–306). Boston, MA: Allyn & Bacon.

Piechowski, M. M. (2006). *Mellow out, they say. If only I could: Intensities and sensitivities of the young and bright.* Madison, WI: Yunasa Books.

Piechowski, M. M. (2014). *Mellow out, they say. If only I could: Intensities and sensitivities of the young and bright* (2nd ed.). Unionville, NY: Royal Fireworks Press.

Piechowski, M. M., & Cunningham, K. (1985). Patterns of overexcitability in a group of artists. *Journal of Creative Behavior, 19,* 153–174.

Piechowski, M. M., & Daniels, S. (2008). *Living with intensity: Understanding the sensitivity, excitability, and emotional development of gifted children, adolescents and adults.* Scottsdale, AZ: Great Potential Press.

Post, G. (2015). *Difficult passage: Gifted girls in middle school* [Web log post]. Retrieved from https://giftedchallenges.blogspot.com/ 2015/05/difficult-passage-gifted-girls-in.html

Renzulli, J. S. (1978) What makes giftedness ? Reexamining a definition. *Phi Delta Kappan, 60,* 180–184, 261.

Roeper, A. (1995). Gifted adults: Their characteristics and emotions. In *Annemarie Roeper: Selected writings and speeches* (pp. 93–108). Minneapolis, MN: Free Spirit.

Roeper, A. (2000). Giftedness is heart and soul. *Gifted Education Communicator, 31*(4), 32–33, 56–58.

Roeper, A. (2004). The qualitative assessment model. *Roeper Review, 26,* 33.

Roeper, A. (2011). *Beyond old age: Essays on living and dying.* Berkeley, CA: Azalea Art.

Rotter, J. B. (1966). Generalized expectations for internal versus external control of reinforcement. *Psychological Monographs: General and Applied, 80*(1), 1–28.

Schultz, R. A., & Delisle, J. R. (2007). *More than a test score: Teens talk about being gifted, talented, or otherwise extra-ordinary.* Minneapolis, MN: Free Spirit.

Schultz, R. A., & Delisle, J. R. (2013). *If I'm so smart, why aren't the answers easy?* Waco, TX: Prufrock Press.

Stanford University (2018). *Stanford offers admission to 2,040 students.* Retrieved from https://news.stanford.edu/2018/03/30/offers-admission-2040-students

Tannenbaum, A. J. (1983). *Gifted children: Psychological and educational perspectives.* New York, NY: Teachers College Press.

Terman, L. M. (1925). *Genetic studies of genius* (Vol. 1). Stanford, CA: Stanford University Press.

Torrance, E. P., Murdock, M., & Fletcher, D. C. (1996). *Creative problem solving through role playing.* Pretoria, Republic of South Africa: Benedic Books.

Vonnegut, K. (2005). *A man without a country.* New York, NY: Seven Stories Press.

Walker, J. (Producer), & Bird, B. (Writer/Director). (2004). *The incredibles* [Motion picture]. United States: Disney/Pixar.

Webb, J. T. (2013). *Searching for meaning: Idealism, bright minds, disillusionment, and hope.* Tucson, AZ: Great Potential Press.

Webb, J. T., Amend, E. R., Beljan, P., Webb, N. E., Kuzujanakis, M., Olenchak, F. R., & Goerss, J. (2016). *Misdiagnosis and dual diagnoses of gifted children and adults: ADHD, bipolar, OCD, Asperger's, depression, and other disorders* (2nd ed.). Tucson, AZ: Great Potential Press.

White, D. (2001). *Philosophy for kids: 40 fun questions that help you wonder about everything!* Waco, TX: Prufrock Press.

White, D. (2005). *The examined life: Advanced philosophy for kids.* Waco, TX: Prufrock Press.

Resources

Gifted Education Journals and Publications

Gifted Child Quarterly
Coeditors: Michael Matthews, University of North Carolina, Charlotte; Jill Adelson, University of Louisville
Website: http://www.nagc.org/resources-publications/ nagc-publications/gifted-child-quarterly

Gifted Child Today
Editor: Susan K. Johnsen, Baylor University
Website: http://journals.sagepub.com/home/gct

Gifted Education Communicator
Editor: Sandra N. Kaplan, University of Southern California
Website: http://giftededucationcommunicator.com

Gifted and Talented International
Coeditors: Leonie Kronborg, Monash University;
Megan Foley-Nicpon, The University of Iowa
Website: https://www.world-gifted.org/publications/
gifted-talented-international

Journal for the Education of the Gifted
Editor: Tracy L. Cross, The Center for Gifted Education,
William & Mary
Website: http://journals.sagepub.com/home/jeg

Parenting for High Potential
Editor: Kathleen Nilles
Website: http://www.nagc.org/parenting-high-potential-1

Roeper Review
Editor: Don Ambrose, Rider University
Website: http://www.tandfonline.com/toc/uror20/current

United States National Gifted Associations and Department of Education

American Association for Gifted Children (AAGC)
E-mail: info@aagc.org
Website: http://www.aagc.org

Council for Exceptional Children (CEC)
E-mail: service@cec.sped.org
Website: https://www.cec.sped.org

The Association for the Gifted, Council for Exceptional Children (CEC-TAG)
E-mail: tlcross@wm.edu
Website: http://www.cectag.org

National Association for Gifted Children (NAGC)
E-mail: nagc@nagc.org
Website: https://www.nagc.org

Supporting the Emotional Needs of the Gifted (SENG)
E-mail: office@sengifted.org
Website: http://www.sengifted.org

U.S. Department of Education
Website: https://www.ed.gov

Centers for Gifted Education

Center for Creative Learning
Don Treffinger, President
E-mail: info@creativelearning.com
Website: http://www.creativelearning.com

The Center for Gifted
Joan Franklin Smutny, Director
Northern Illinois University
E-mail: info@centerforgifted.org
Website: http://www.centerforgifted.org

Jodie Mahony Center for Gifted Education
Ann Robinson, Director
University of Arkansas at Little Rock
E-mail: aerobinson@ualr.edu
Website: http://ualr.edu/gifted

Center for Gifted Education
Christine Briggs, Director
University of Louisiana at Lafayette
E-mail: gifted@louisiana.edu
Website: https://curriculum.louisiana.edu/about-us/centers/
center-gifted-education

Center for Gifted Education
Jann Leppien, Director
Whitworth College
E-mail: gifted@whitworth.edu
Website: https://www.whitworth.edu/cms/academics/
graduate-studies-in-education/center-for-gifted-education

Center for Gifted Education
Tracy L. Cross, Executive Director
William & Mary
E-mail: cfge@wm.edu
Website: http://education.wm.edu/centers/cfge

The Center for Gifted Education
Mary Potthoff, Director
Drury University
E-mail: mpotthof@drury.edu
Website: http://www.drury.edu/gifted-education

The Center for Gifted Studies
Julia Roberts, Executive Director
Western Kentucky University
E-mail: gifted@wku.edu
Website: https://www.wku.edu/gifted

Center for Gifted Studies and Talent Development
Krista Stith, Director
Ball State University
E-mail: giftedcenter@bsu.edu
Website: https://www.bsu.edu/gifted

Center for Talent Development
Paula Olszewski-Kubilius, Director
Northwestern University
E-mail: ctd@northwestern.edu
Website: https://www.ctd.northwestern.edu

Center for Talented Youth (CTY)
Elaine Tuttle Hansen, Executive Director
Johns Hopkins University
E-mail: ctyinfo@jhu.edu
Website: https://www.jhu.edu/gifted

DISCOVER Projects
C. June Maker, Director
University of Arizona
E-mail: coe-discover@email.arizona.edu
Website: http://discover.arizona.edu

Duke University Talent Identification Program (TIP)
Shawna Young, Executive Director
Duke University
E-mail: inquiries@tip.duke.edu
Website: https://www.tip.duke.edu

Frances A. Karnes Center for Gifted Studies
Heather L. Houston, Director
The University of Southern Mississippi
E-mail: giftedstudies@usm.edu
Website: https://www.usm.edu/karnes-gifted

Gifted Development Center
Linda Kreger Silverman
E-mail: gifted@gifteddevelopment.com
Website: http://www.gifteddevelopment.com

Gifted Education Resource Institute (GERI)
Marcia Gentry, Director
Purdue University
E-mail: geri@purdue.edu
Website: https://www.education.purdue.edu/geri

The Hollingworth Center
Lisa Wright and James Borland, Directors
Teachers College, Columbia University
E-mail: hollingworth@tc.edu
Website: https://www.tc.columbia.edu/hollingworth

Institute for Educational Advancement
Betsy Jones, President
Website: https://www.educationaladvancement.org

**Renzulli Center for Creativity, Gifted
Education, and Talent Development**
Joseph Renzulli, Director
University of Connecticut
E-mail: judith.mathews@uconn.edu
Website: https://www.gifted.uconn.edu

Torrance Center for Creativity and Talent Development
Sarah Sumners, Director
University of Georgia
E-mail: creative@uga.edu
Website: https://www.coe.uga.edu/Torrance

Helpful Websites

National Association for Gifted Children
https://www.nagc.org

**Acceleration Institute: *A Nation Deceived*
(2004) and *A Nation Empowered* (2015)**
http://www.accelerationinstitute.org/nation_deceived

Hoagies' Gifted Education Page
http://www.hoagiesgifted.org

Davidson Institute for Talent Development
http://www.davidsongifted.org

GT World
https://www.gtworld.org

State Associations and Departments of Education Websites

Alabama Association for Gifted Children (AAGC)
http://www.alabamagifted.org

Alaska Department of Education and Early Development
https://education.alaska.gov

Arizona Association for Gifted and Talented
http://arizonagifted.org

Arizona Department of Education, Gifted Education
http://www.azed.gov/gifted-education

Arkansas Department of Education
http://www.arkansased.gov

California Association for the Gifted (CAG)
https://www.cagifted.org

California Department of Education, Gifted and Talented Education (GATE)
https://www.cde.ca.gov/sp/gt

Colorado Association for Gifted and Talented
http://www.coloradogifted.org

Colorado Department of Education, Office of Gifted Education
http://www.cde.state.co.us/gt

Connecticut Association for the Gifted (CAG)
http://www.ctgifted.org

Connecticut State Department of Education, Gifted and Talented
http://portal.ct.gov/SDE/Gifted-and-Talented

Delaware Department of Education
https://www.doe.k12.de.us

District of Columbia Office of the State Superintendent of Education
https://osse.dc.gov

Florida Association for the Gifted (FLAG)
http://www.flagifted.org

Florida Gifted Network
https://www.floridagiftednetwork.org

Georgia Association for Gifted Children
http://www.gagc.org

Hawaii State Department of Education
http://www.hawaiipublicschools.org

Idaho: The Association for the Gifted/State Advocates for Gifted Education (ITAG/SAGE)
http://itagsage.org

Idaho State Department of Education, Gifted and Talented
https://www.sde.idaho.gov/academic/gifted-talented

Illinois Association for Gifted Children
http://www.iagcgifted.org

Indiana Association for the Gifted (IAG)
http://www.iag-online.org

Indiana Department of Education, Office of High Ability Education
https://www.doe.in.gov/highability

Iowa Talented and Gifted Association (ITAG)
http://iowatag.org

Kansas Association for Gifted, Talented, and Creative
http://www.kgtc.org

Kentucky Association for Gifted Education (KAGE)
http://kagegifted.org

Louisiana Department of Education, Gifted and Talented
https://www.louisianabelieves.com/academics/gifted-and-talented-students

Maine Department of Education
http://www11.maine.gov/doe

Gifted and Talented Association of Montgomery County, Maryland
https://gtamc.org

Maryland State Department of Education
http://www.marylandpublicschools.org/Pages/default.aspx

Massachusetts Association for Gifted Education (MAGE)
http://www.massgifted.org

Michigan Association for Gifted Children
http://www.migiftedchild.org

Minnesota Council for the Gifted and Talented
http://www.mcgt.net

Mississippi Department of Education, Advanced Learning and Gifted Programs
http://www.mde.k12.ms.us/ESE/ALGP

Gifted Association of Missouri (GAM)
http://www.mogam.org

Missouri Department of Elementary and Secondary Education, Gifted Education
https://dese.mo.gov/quality-schools/gifted-education

Montana Association of Gifted and Talented Education (AGATE)
http://www.mtagate.org

Nebraska Association for the Gifted
http://negifted.org

State of Nevada Department of Education
http://www.doe.nv.gov

New Hampshire Association for Gifted Education (NHAGE)
http://www.nhage.org

New Jersey Association for Gifted Children (NJAGC)
http://www.njagc.org

New Mexico Public Education Department
http://webnew.ped.state.nm.us

New York City Department of Education, Gifted and Talented
https://schools.nyc.gov/ChoicesEnrollment/GiftedandTalented/
default.htm

North Carolina Association for the Gifted and Talented (NCAGT)
http://www.ncagt.org

Public Schools of North Carolina, Exceptional Children
https://ec.ncpublicschools.gov

North Dakota Department of Public Instruction
http://www.dpi.state.nd.us

Ohio Association for Gifted Children (OAGC)
http://www.oagc.com

Ohio Department of Education, Gifted Education
http://education.ohio.gov/Topics/Other-Resources/
Gifted-Education

**Oklahoma Association for the Gifted,
Creative, and Talented (OAGCT)**
https://www.oagct.org

Oklahoma State Department of Education, Gifted and Talented
http://sde.ok.gov/sde/gifted-and-talented-education

Oregon Association for Talented and Gifted (OATAG)
http://www.oatag.org

Pennsylvania Association for Gifted Education (PAGE)
https://www.giftedpage.org

Pennsylvania Department of Education
http://www.education.pa.gov/Pages/default.aspx

Rhode Island Advocates for Gifted Education (RIAGE)
http://www.riage.org

Rhode Island Department of Education
http://www.ride.ri.gov

South Carolina Department of Education, Gifted and Talented
https://ed.sc.gov/instruction/standards-learning/
advanced-academic-programs/gifted-and-talented

Tennessee Association for the Gifted (TAG)
http://www.tag-tenn.org

Texas Association for the Gifted and Talented (TAGT)
https://www.txgifted.org

Texas Education Agency, Special Student Populations
https://tea.texas.gov/Academics/Special_Student_Populations

Utah Association for Gifted Children (UAGC)
https://www.uagc.org

Utah State Board of Education, Gifted and Talented
https://www.schools.utah.gov/curr/giftedtalented

Vermont Talent Development Institute
https://tdivermont.org

Virginia Association for the Gifted
http://www.vagifted.org

Virginia Department of Education, Gifted Education
http://www.doe.virginia.gov/instruction/gifted_ed

**Washington Association of Educators of the
Talented and Gifted (WAETAG)**
http://www.waetag.net

West Virginia Association for Gifted and Talented (WVAGT)
http://www.wvgifted.com

**West Virginia Department of Education,
Office of Special Education**
http://wvde.state.wv.us/osp

Wisconsin Association for Talented and Gifted (WATG)
http://www.watg.org

**Wisconsin Department of Public Instruction,
Division for Academic Excellence**
http://www.dpi.wi.gov/dae

Wyoming Department of Education
https://edu.wyoming.gov

Canadian Gifted Education Resources

Canadian Council for Exceptional Children
http://community.cec.sped.org/canada/home

Alberta Associations for Bright Children (AABC)
http://www.edmontonabc.org/aabc

Gifted Children's Association of British Columbia
https://giftedchildrenbc.org

Manitoba Education and Training
http://www.edu.gov.mb.ca

Newfoundland and Labrador, Gifted and Talented
http://www.ed.gov.nl.ca/edu/k12/studentsupportservices/gifted.html

The Association for Bright Children (ABC) of Ontario
http://www.abcontario.ca

Prince Edward Island Department of Education
https://www.princeedwardisland.ca/en/topic/
education-early-learning-and-culture

Ministère de l'Éducation/Education Québec
http://www.education.gouv.qc.ca/en/
ministere-de-leducation-et-de-lenseignement-superieur

Saskatchewan Education and Learning
https://www.saskatchewan.ca/residents/education-and-learning

Saskatchewan Teachers' Federation Resources
https://www.stf.sk.ca/professional-resources/
stewart-resources-centre/resources

**Government of the Northwest Territories:
Education, Culture, and Employment**
http://www.ece.gov.nt.ca

Nunavut Department of Education
https://www.gov.nu.ca/education

Yukon Government, Department of Education
http://www.education.gov.yk.ca

About the Author

James R. Delisle, Ph.D., has taught gifted children and those who work on their behalf for more than 40 years. He retired from Kent State University after 25 years of service as a professor of special education. He is the author of more than 275 articles and 21 books, and his work has been translated into multiple languages and featured in both professional journals and popular media. Jim currently teaches part-time at Scholars Academy, a high school for highly gifted students in Conway, SC.

Printed in the United States
by Baker & Taylor Publisher Services